What Your Colleagues Are

This is the book PBL educators have been waiting for! Whether you are starting out on your PBL journey or have been at it for years, this book is full of helpful ideas, tactics, and exemplars—the kind of book that never even makes it to the shelf because you are constantly using it. Jennifer Pieratt knows how to help educators realize their own potential to facilitate powerful PBL experiences for all students. This book is a window into her years of expertise and experiences.

—Emily Liebtag, Vice President, Advocacy
Getting Smart

For someone new to teaching or to project-based learning, this workbook simplifies the process without letting go of essential elements that make the project a valuable educational experience.

—Marcia LeCompte, Retired Montessori Teacher
Dufrocq Elementary School, Baton Rouge, LA

This book is an excellent tool for any educator wanting to implement project-based learning in their classroom. It provides a step-by-step guide that takes you through the thought process—from posing the question for the project, to the planning that is involved before implementing the project, the process for implementing the project, assessment of the project, and the background resources needed to begin the process.

—Ellen Asregadoo, Teacher
Public School 190, Brooklyn, NY

It is inspiring to see how our students can make a positive impact on our world when we as educators empower them through project-based learning. This book provides the necessary structures, supports, and encouragement to shift to these dynamic practices so that we can better serve all learners. I have witnessed firsthand the incredible transformation when educators shift practice to embrace the complexities of real-world challenges, and I am excited that this resource will help to spread these powerful learning opportunities to better serve all learners.

—Devin Vodicka, Superintendent and Chief Impact Officer
AltSchool, Oceanside, CA

In her introduction to Keep It Real With PBL, Jenny Pieratt describes her commitment to be direct with teachers about developing engaging and strong PBL experiences for their students. She has done just that, combining her deep experience from varied perspectives—PBL teacher and colleague, coach, consultant—to provide a straightforward but detailed path to developing high quality PBL opportunities for learners. Jenny is at once optimistic and realistic, encouraging and pragmatic. While this book is designed for teachers just starting out in PBL work, experienced PBL teachers will benefit from the thoroughness of Jenny's descriptions of planning and implementing strong PBL experiences—and will almost surely be introduced to useful new resources as well.

—Rick Lear, Former Senior Director for
School Design and Implementation, New Tech Network
Former Interim Executive Director, Envision Learning Partners

KEEP IT REAL with PBL

KEEP IT REAL

WITH PBL

A Practical Guide for
PLANNING
PROJECT-BASED
LEARNING

SECONDARY

JENNIFER PIERATT

FOR INFORMATION:

Corwin

A SAGE Company

2455 Teller Road

Thousand Oaks, California 91320

(800) 233-9936

www.corwin.com

SAGE Publications Ltd.

1 Oliver's Yard

55 City Road

London EC1Y 1SP

United Kingdom

SAGE Publications India Pvt. Ltd.

B 1/I 1 Mohan Cooperative Industrial Area

Mathura Road, New Delhi 110 044

India

SAGE Publications Asia-Pacific Pte. Ltd.

18 Cross Street #10-10/11/12

China Square Central

Singapore 048423

Printed in the United States of America

ISBN 978-1-5443-6937-2

Acquisitions Editor: Ariel Curry

Development Editor: Desirée A. Bartlett

Associate Content

   Development Editor: Jessica Vidal

Project Editor: Amy Schroller

Copy Editor: Amy Hanquist Harris

Typesetter: C&M Digitals (P) Ltd.

Proofreader: Dennis W. Webb

Indexer: Jean Casalegno

Cover Designer: Gail Buschman

Marketing Manager: Margaret O'Connor

This book is printed on acid-free paper.

20 21 22 23 24 10 9 8 7 6 5 4 3 2 1

Contents

Visit the companion website at
resources.corwin.com/keepitrealPBLsecondary
for downloadable resources.

Note From the Publisher: The author has provided video and web content throughout the book that is available to you through QR (quick response) codes. To read a QR code, you must have a smartphone or tablet with a camera. We recommend that you download a QR code reader app that is made specifically for your phone or tablet brand.

Videos may also be accessed at **resources.corwin.com/keepitrealPBLsecondary**

List of Resources on the Companion Website

Chapter 1

- The Main Course, Not Dessert
- Problem-Based Learning (PrBL)
  - "'Isn't Problem-Based Learning Easier Than Project-Based Learning" and 10 Other Myths About PrBL
- P21 Framework
  - Creativity and Innovation
  - Critical Thinking and Problem-Solving
  - Communication
  - Collaboration
  - High-Quality PBL (HQPBL)
  - New Tech Network Project Quality Checklist
  - EL Education Models of Excellence
  - PBLWorks Gold-Standard PBL: Essential Project Design Elements
  - [VIDEO] *Simon Sinek: The Golden Circle*
- Differentiation, Equity in PBL
  - Inclusive Special Education via PBL
  - Project-Based Learning With an Equity Lens
  - Promising Practices in Equity and Project-Based Learning
  - Ensuring PBL That Is Accessible to All

Chapter 2

- Collegial Pedagogy
- Learning as Production, Critique as Assessment by Lissa Soep
- Teaching Is a Project-Based Profession: Ten PBL Teacher Mindsets by Emily Liebtag
- Agency (Adult and Student) in PBL
  - Agency and High-Quality PBL by Marie Bjerede
  - New Tech Network Agency Rubric, Grade 5
  - [VIDEO] *The Power of Belief: Mindset and Success* by Eduardi Briceno
  - [VIDEO] *Grit: The Power of Passion and Perseverance* by Angela Duckworth
  - Why Mindset Matters by Marina Krakovsky

Chapter 3

- Project Brainstorming Protocols and Critical Friends
  - The Wagon Wheel Protocol From NSRF
  - The Carousel Protocol From Expeditionary Learning
  - The Tuning Protocol From School 21

- o   The Tuning Protocol From the School Reform Initiative
- o   Critical Friends: Building a Culture of Collaboration by Jenny Pieratt

Chapter 4

- Math PrBL Pacing Guides
- Examples of Power Standards:
  - o   Washington State Standards
  - o   Science Content Standards for California Public Schools, K–12
  - o   History–Social Science Standards for California Public Schools, K–12
  - o   [PPT] Identifying Essential Standards
  - o   Prioritizing the Common Core Power Standards
  - o   Priority Standards: The Power of Focus

Chapter 5

- Infographics: Deeper Learning Lesson
- Infographics as a Benchmark Within a Project
- Using Infographics to Drive Deep Learning
- Bring Authentic Learning to Life With Infographics
- Visible Thinking Core Routines
- Seven-Minute Project Tuning
- Project Prune From *Going Online With Protocols*
- I Like, I Wish, What If

Chapter 6

- "Teacher Tech Tools" is a website created for teachers by a fifth-grade teacher, Camille Nunnenkamp, to help them feel both comfortable and inspired to leverage technology in their classrooms. Teacher Tech Tools houses grade-level specific sample projects in which technology is used to assess students' evaluation and creation skills within a project. Each project example includes a step-by-step tutorial of the application or technological platform used for easy implementation in your classroom.

Chapter 7

- NGSS Assessment
  - o   Designing Assessments for Formative Use
  - o   NGSS Evidence Statements
  - o   Creating Rubrics for Performance Tasks
  - o   Rubrics for Classroom Science Assessment
  - o   Cross-Cutting Concepts for Middle School Students
  - o   California NGSS Early Implementation Initiative
  - o   Meet the #SinglePointRubric
  - o   Your Rubric Is a Hot Mess. Here's How to Fix It.

Chapter 9

- Protocols:
  - o   EL Education: Classroom Protocols
  - o   Expeditionary Learning Teacher Resources

- Professional Development-Sustaining HQPBL
  - Scaling PBL: Three Steps for Defining Quality With Your Staff
  - Five Steps for Sustaining PBL

Lenses for Looking at Student Work

- New Tech Network's Project Quality Checklist
- The PBLWorks Essential Project Design Elements Checklist
- Expeditionary Learning's Attributes of High-Quality Work
- Getting Smart's HQPBL Framework

Exemplar Projects

- PBLU Pick a Project
- Models of Excellence: The Center for High-Quality Student Work
- High Tech High Student Projects
- Deeper Learning Lesson
- DreamUp Space Curriculum

General PBL Resources

- Teacher Talks Podcast: PBL With Jenny Pieratt, *Teaching Channel*
- God Save the Routine: Debunking Five PBL Myths, *ASCD*
- Assessment and Other Dirty Words in PBL, *Teaching Channel*
- Three Simple Steps to Project Ideation, *Teaching Channel*
- Deciding When PBL Makes Sense for Your Year, *Teaching Channel*
- Small but Mighty: Voice and Choice in PBL, *Teaching Channel*
- Getting Ready for the PBL Paradigm Shift, *Getting Smart*
- Differentiation in PBL, *PBLWorks*
- The Power of Collaboration in PBL, *Project Foundry*
- Using Infographics in PBL, *Infogram*
- Getting Started With Place-Based Learning, *Getting Smart*
- Using Infographics to Get to Deeper Learning, *Piktochart*
- Deeper Learning Through BYOD, *EdSurge*
- Real-World Work and Career Readiness, *P21*
- Three Steps to Successful Student Collaboration, *Teaching Channel*
- Five Tips for Painless Prototyping, *ASCD*

Appendix A: Complete Project Plans

Appendix B: Blank Project Templates

Appendix C: Teacher Toolbox

Acknowledgments

People often ask how I first got involved in PBL, and I always smile thinking of my eighth-grade student, Michael D. Thank you to Michael for teaching me about PBL, being the first to believe in me, and nudging me to go find my people.

To the secondary teachers who are facing so many barriers in this work but who continue to fight to find ways to make it work, especially the maverick PBL teachers at AOMS and CHMS in Carlsbad, California; to those whose work is featured in this book—Kate Therriault, Aaron Sottile, Jen Stillittano, Gifford Asimos, Ashley Crawford, Leslie Frazee, Nicole Moersh, and Beth Riis; and to my forever friends and colleagues of High Tech High North County: Thank you for sharing your projects, quotes, feedback, and your continued support of my work.

Thank you to the entire editorial team at Corwin, in particular the design team who executed my crazy (chicken scratch) ideas and made this book beautiful.

While there were many people who supported me in my PBL journey and in writing this book, I would like to acknowledge the incredible men in my life.

Thank you to a few prominent mentors: Rick Lear, Rob Riordan, Jim May, Isaac Jones, and Jacob Adams—I cherish every thoughtful conversation we had. To my two dads, thank you for your incredible model of hard work and passion; I hope you can see it bleed through this book! And Mike, Papa Mendes, and Papa Ray—thank you for reminding me to always keep my eye on what matters most.

Thank you to my husband, Greg. I believe the definition of a man is one who can stand beside a woman, but a *real* man is just as proud to stand *behind* her—thank you for being that for me. I adore that you know every acronym in this book and can speak about every school I have touched. Your love, support, loyalty, and encouragement have never gone unnoticed.

And to my son, Landon: Thank you for every time you ask about my work and also for every time you ask me to *stop* my work to play with you in the street or at the fields—you have given me the gift of presence and perspective. I hope I have instilled in you the drive to dream big, work hard, and cheer wildly when you achieve. May we always be each other's number-one fans; thank you for being mine throughout this journey.

Publisher's Acknowledgments

Corwin gratefully acknowledges the contributions of the following reviewers:

Ellen Asregadoo
Fifth-Grade Teacher
Public School 190
Brooklyn, NY

Randy Cook
Science Teacher
Howard City, MI

Christine Landwehrle
Assistant Superintendent
Amherst, NH

Marcia LeCompte
Retired Montessori Teacher
Dufrocq Elementary School
Baton Rouge, LA

Kelley S. Miller
Academic Specialist, Grades 6–8
Silverado Middle School
Napa, CA

Ernie Rambo
Virtual Learning Community Coordinator/
Professional Learning Facilitator
Nevada National Board Professional Learning
Institute
Las Vegas, NV

Roshani Shah
Seventh-Grade Gifted/Accelerated Math
Summerour Middle School
Norcross, GA

Stephanie L. Turner
Fourth-Grade General Education Teacher
Bradley Academy—An Arts Integrated School
Murfreesboro, TN

Peggy Williams
English, Speech, Psychology, and Sociology
Teacher
Grades 10–12
Humboldt-Table Rock-Steinauer Public Schools
Humboldt, NE

About the Author

Jennifer (Jenny) Pieratt, PhD, is a progressive educator and teacherpreneur. She was a founding staff member at High Tech High North County, a former school development coach at New Tech Network, and National Faculty at PBLWorks. In 2016, Jenny became the founder and president of CraftED—a leading voice for the "mainstream wave" of PBL implementation through virtual and onsite professional development and coaching, active networking, and practitioner-based publications. With a PhD in educational philosophy, specifically PBL, Jenny prides herself on staying in the trenches with teachers and advocating for teacher support to bring HQPBL to classrooms across the United States. Jenny is an active blogger and speaker, a former teacher of Grades 5–10, equity advocate, and proud small business owner. Jenny resides in Cardiff-by-the-Sea, California, with her husband and two children.

Introduction

Letter to Secondary Teachers

This workbook reflects the project-planning process I have developed from my experience in the trenches of project-based learning (PBL) over the past decade. From my time as a founding teacher at High Tech High North County to serving as a school development coach for New Tech Network and national faculty member of PBLWorks, I know firsthand how challenging designing projects can be, especially for secondary teachers with large caseloads of students and short class periods to engage in meaningful teaching and learning. When I set out to support teachers independently through my company, CraftED, I committed to honoring the reality every secondary teacher faces: standards, assessment, the need for structure, the lack of resources to implement PBL, and the lack of collaborative planning time with colleagues.

Too often there is a disconnect between the romantic ideals of PBL and the real challenges that are in front of teachers—a classroom full of 25 to 30 students with diverse needs, multiple "preps" in your schedule, dwindling amounts of planning time, a caseload of 150 students, district pacing guides, lack of resources, and forever-changing curriculum implementation. I became inspired by the notion that my close (nonteacher) friend offered up when she said, "Hey, I just did a quick search on Twitter of that PBL thing you keep talking about, and it seems like there are a lot of 'pains' related to PBL. I know you well enough to know that people love you when you are raw, so give them what they want—just keep it real, girl." And so began my personal PBL #realtalk campaign—no fancy frameworks, no more jargon, no more ignoring the challenges and fears of teachers being asked to do this work. I WANT TO KEEP IT REAL!

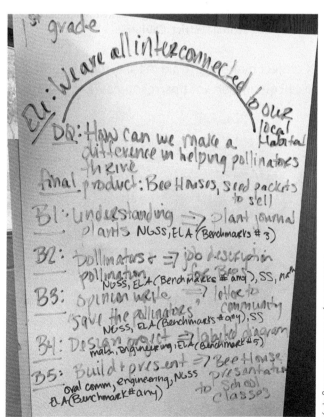

● **FIGURE 0.1** Jenny's previous project-planning process

Photo courtesy of Chris Nelson Photography.

● **FIGURE 0.2** Jenny presenting at Lake Elementary, Vista Unified School District, California

The first step of my #realtalk mission was to address head-on that while planning frameworks can be helpful, they also can be overwhelming—especially when they are multiple pages long! When I worked for PBL organizations, I was provided resources to support teachers with project planning. Truth be told, though, I never used them; I always "went rogue." So I attempted to codify how I held teachers' hands in the planning process. For two years, that process worked, but it was pretty ugly. Teachers would leave my planning sessions with large poster papers or whiteboard snapshots covered with my signature umbrella arch, chicken scratch writing, and tons of arrows and sticky notes (see Figures 0.1 and 0.2). This book is an attempt to tidy up that planning process so teachers can document it in a clearer and more efficient way.

How to Use This Book

This book is designed to be interactive and support teachers through the iterative process of project planning. To aid in this process, there are several icons incorporated throughout the book to call out important tips, resources, and tools:

 #realtalk sound bites that honor the challenges to implementing PBL.

 Key terminology and acronyms in PBL.

 Tips and resources to support the project planning process.

 Exercises to help you reflect and process throughout your project plans.

 Planning forms to guide you through planning your project.

Chapter 1
The What and Why of Project-Based Learning

An Overview of Project-Based Learning (PBL)

Project-based learning (PBL) is one of many trends currently sweeping across the educational landscape, hoping to revolutionize how students learn. Despite being dressed up as a new and innovative approach to teaching and learning, PBL has actually been around, in a variety of forms, since the turn of the twentieth century. Dating back to the work of great progressive thinkers such as John Dewey, Vygotsky, and Piaget (Pieratt, 2011), PBL is hardly new. In *Experience and Education*, Dewey (1938) laid the foundation for PBL by explaining that when learning is relevant to the world and the experiences of the child, education becomes more meaningful and thus engaging.

A leading organization of PBL, PBLWorks, defines *PBL* as [an experience in which]

> students are pulled through the curriculum by a meaningful question to explore, an engaging real-world problem to solve, or a challenge to design or create something. . . . To demonstrate what they learn, students create high-quality products to present their work to other people. (Hallermann, Larmer, & Mergendoller, 2011, p. 5)

PBL can occur in any school setting (home, public, charter, private, etc.) and at any grade level (preK–higher education).

PBL typically includes the following:

- Teacher-designed learning experiences related to grade-level standards
- A real-world connection to classroom learning, such as community issues with local audiences
- Hands-on and active learning activities
- Student engagement, as a result of the integration of student interests
- A focus on twenty-first century skills (such as collaboration or oral communication)
- Incorporation, possibly full integration, of a variety of content areas
- Assessments throughout the project with feedback and reflection

#realtalk: "PBLs" isn't a thing. Project-based learning is a way of teaching and learning—it is not singular, and it is not plural; it is an ongoing and comprehensive mode of instruction (pedagogy). If you want to talk about more than one project, you can call it "PBL units" or "PBL projects," but please not PBLs!

While this list is not exhaustive, it may begin to provide you with a more vivid picture of what project-based learning looks like in action. To deepen this knowledge, it is helpful to understand the many ways in which PBL is different from the traditional approach to teaching and learning:

- The role of the teacher shifts to a *facilitator* of learning. In PBL, lessons are not traditional in nature. Although teachers may "stand and deliver" a lecture or a small lesson here and there, they are more commonly *orchestrating* the execution of their well-thought-out plans for student discovery during the actual class time with students.

- Because students are often exploring "real-time" issues, the teacher and student often *learn together*. In this same vein, textbooks are rare in PBL because the content is quickly outdated for what students are learning in the project.

- Students often display more *ownership* over their learning, including task management, because of the process of a project.

- Regardless of age or content, students are frequently provided opportunities to develop a variety of twenty-first century skills, such as *collaboration* and *communication*.

- PBL is *flexible*, meaning the framework allows teachers and students to be responsive to student and community needs and interests.

- Assessment is frequent throughout a project and includes *feedback* from the teacher mid-project so that the student has opportunities to grow over the course of the project. PBL is action-oriented, meaning students are expected to *DO* something with their knowledge by applying it or inspiring others to do something.

- PBL pushes beyond rote memorization and requires students to *dig deeper* in their learning and think through application and innovation of new ideas/solutions.

It is critical to understand the difference between a project and PBL as a pedagogy. Check out *The Main Course, not Dessert: How Are Students Reaching 21st Century Goals? With 21st Century Project Based Learning* by Larmer and Mergendoller (2010). In it, the authors use the analogy of a main course (the "meaty" learning that happens in the middle) and dessert (the fluffy project that happens after all the learning occurs) to talk about this important difference. You can find the link to it on our companion website (resources .corwin.com/keepitrealPBLsecondary).

PrBL Versus PBL

What are the differences between problem-based learning (PrBL) and PBL? In *Necessary Conditions*, math expert Geoff Krall (2018) explains:

> Similar to problem-based learning, project-based learning ties the content to a real world context by providing the challenge

that makes the math content necessary. The key differences between the two are the length of time required and the level of authenticity [or real-world connectedness]. (p. 87)

Figure 1.1 is a helpful diagram to show the main differences between these two similar yet different pedagogies: While a problem or series of problems may be incorporated into a project, PBL has fundamentally different characteristics—namely, focusing on process and product, and increased number of standards and time dedicated to learning.

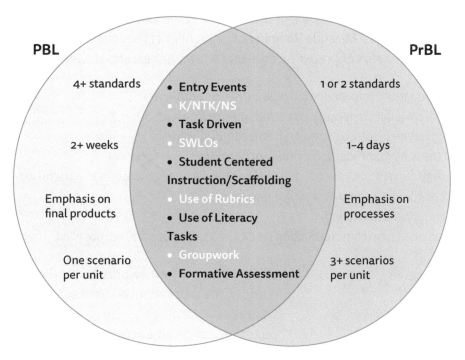

● **FIGURE 1.1** PBL versus PrBL

Source: Geoff Krall, used with permission.

Why PBL?

So if PBL has been around for a century, what seems to be driving the mainstream momentum of this pedagogy sweeping across our schools?

Workforce Readiness

The U.S. Department of Education writes,

> There is growing consensus that America's students need to be prepared to compete in a world that demands more than just basic skills. Today, about a third of American students require remedial education when

Tip: **If you are a math, science, or foreign language teacher interested in PBL, you may consider starting first with designing a problem-based learning unit to prepare you for diving into PBL. You may find that PrBL gets to some important shifts in student-centered learning (inquiry, problem-solving, collaboration, communication, agency, etc.), while providing a balance of content coverage and practice with specific skills.**

they enter college, and current college attainment rates are not keeping pace with our country's projected workforce needs. (n.d., para. 3)

This concern, shared by many educators, policy makers, and prominent business figures, led to the development of the P21 framework. The framework outlines the following outcomes as twenty-first century skills that schools should be fostering within students: creativity and innovation, critical thinking and problem-solving, communication, and collaboration. More information on these individual skills can be found on the companion website. While many pedagogical theories may address *some* of these skills, PBL often serves as a favored vehicle for addressing all of these skills. Miranda Reagan (2015) highlights the following ways in which PBL offers the additional benefits of preparing students with other essential twenty-first century skills:

- *Creativity (applying knowledge to solve authentic problems)*
- *Collaboration (effectively and respectfully interacting with others)*
- *Communication (listening, speaking, and combining ideas)*
- *Critical thinking (approaching a problem from a fresh perspective)*
- *Technology application (discovering and applying new technologies in a useful way)*
- *Analytical applied writing (writing for a purpose)*
- *Growth mindset (risk-taking)*
- *Authentic audience (communicating results in a way that gives purpose to learning)*

#realtalk: PBL (project-based learning), PrBL (problem-based learning), DTK (design thinking), IB (International Baccalaureate), CGI (cognitively guided instruction), IQB (inquiry-based learning), STEM (science, technology, engineering, math)—put 'em together and you have buzz-phrase acronym soup! Each of these frameworks provides a unique approach to teaching and learning, and with each of these comes its own host of pros and cons. It's important to think about why you are choosing PBL over one of these other frameworks for your students. And if you are choosing to combine multiple frameworks, consider how you will uphold fidelity of each of those unique instructional approaches.

Of the variety of frameworks currently in schools, PBL is one of the more robust—both in structure and time. Because all learning happens within the course of a project, it can be all-encompassing, meaning it is large enough to apply, scaffold, and assess a variety of skills (and content) over the course of completing a project.

Innovation

Often connected to workforce readiness is innovation, or the idea of developing our graduates into change agents who will help keep our country competitive in the global marketplace. In a 2018 report, the United States fell out of the top-10 list, ranking 11th among innovative countries (Jamrisko & Lu, 2018). With economic and political implications tied to innovation, a growing sense of urgency is building to rethink what and how students are learning in school. Tony Wagner (2015) writes,

With well-designed pedagogy, we can empower kids with critical skills and help them turn passions into decisive life advantages. The role of education is no longer to teach content, but to help our children learn—in a world that rewards the innovative and punishes the formulaic. (para. 10)

As a result, schools are thinking deeply about how they can foster innovators. Because PBL is grounded in the creation of a student-developed product, it is a framework that easily fosters creativity, ingenuity, and problem-solving while also upholding the rigor of content expectations.

Student Achievement

Data from 2015 PISA international math and science assessments indicated that U.S. students continue to rank around the middle of the pack and behind many other advanced industrial nations (DeSilver, 2017). And with performance data publicly available, it is a topic at the forefront of every teacher and school leader's mind.

John Hattie conducted a study in 2014 that looked at the effectiveness of factors in teaching and learning. And while he did not look specifically at PBL, he did look at critical components that make up PBL and pointed to them as being highly effective for improving student learning, including feedback, building on prior knowledge, and questioning. Larmer (2016a) writes about Hattie's findings:

> Good teaching is not merely to know how to use specific instructional techniques, but when to use what approach, and to mix and match in service of student learning. Hattie writes that good teaching "combines, rather than contrasts, teacher-centered teaching and student-centered learning and knowing." Projects provide fertile opportunities to do this, pulling together disparate instructional practices—cooperative learning, didactic instruction, peer tutoring, the meta-cognitive strategies of student planning and self-monitoring, woven together with regular formative evaluation and feedback. (paras. 12–13)

So while there are many small moves teachers can make to improve student learning, PBL provides a promising framework to drive such practices. There are a variety of other reasons why PBL continues to gain interest by school leaders and teachers—from new standards (CCSS and NGSS) that lend themselves to real-world application to engaging disenfranchised students through voice and choice in projects.

Intro to HQPBL

As PBL moves away from progressive pockets and becomes a more mainstream pedagogical practice, there is an increasing danger in diluting this approach to teaching and learning. Eager to hop on the PBL bandwagon, schools may claim to adopt PBL without the necessary training, support, and structures to successfully engage in this work. For example, under the guise of "student driven," teachers will often take a hands-off approach to teaching. Without calibration and reflection on this term within PBL, students can be left without critical direction and structures needed to make it a successful teaching and learning methodology. For this reason, there is a pressing need to uphold fidelity to quality.

Leading PBL organizations such as PBLWorks, New Tech Network, High Tech High, and Expeditionary Learning have created their own definition of quality PBL; however, in 2018 a steering committee was created to develop the framework for high-quality project-based learning

(HQPBL), which attempts to take these many existing definitions of exemplar projects and distill them into basic principles. The HQPBL framework includes the following:

- *Intellectual challenge and accomplishment.* Students learn deeply, think critically, and strive for excellence.
- *Authenticity.* Students work on projects that are meaningful and relevant to their culture, their lives, and their future.
- *Public product.* Students' work is publicly displayed, discussed, and critiqued.
- *Collaboration.* Students collaborate with other students in person or online and/or receive guidance from adult mentors and experts.
- *Project management.* Students use a project management process that enables them to proceed effectively from project initiation to completion.
- *Reflection.* Students reflect on their work and their learning throughout the project.

To learn more about this collaborative effort, visit the companion website at resources.corwin.com/ keepitrealPBLsecondary.

#realtalk: While these definitions, checklists, and frameworks are helpful for teacher calibration of quality and continuous improvement, it is important to focus on what matters most to *you* and *your students*. Pick one of these components of quality to focus on in your first project and then continue to build on other layers of quality as you reiterate and improve.

As John Dewey (1938) once said, "The belief that all genuine education comes about through experience does not mean that all experiences are genuinely or equally educative." This is a powerful reminder that while PBL can be a transformative engine for teaching and learning, it must uphold quality to ensure deeper learning.

As you move forward in your project planning, continue to come back to your *why* for PBL—why is it the mode you choose for your instruction for your students?

Journal: Check out this video by Simon Sinek (2009) on the Golden Circle framework to help you understand your *why* for PBL. After viewing, reflect on why you think PBL could be a promising framework for your students.

To read a QR code, you must have a smartphone or tablet with a camera. We recommend that you download a QR code reader app that is made specifically for your phone or tablet brand.

 Video can also be accessed at resources.corwin.com/keepitrealPBLsecondary

If you are thinking to yourself that this sounds great in theory but that your students don't have the skills and they just aren't ready to do PBL yet, know that you are not alone. This is a common concern among teachers of all grades, serving all demographics of students. In *Culturally Responsive Teaching and the Brain*, Zaretta Hammond (2015) explains (related to the widening achievement gap between African American, Latino, and White students) that we often do the following:

But they aren't ready!

- Underestimate what disadvantaged students are intellectually capable of doing
- Postpone more challenging and interesting work until we believe they have mastered "the basics"
- Deprive students of meaningful and motivating context for learning and practicing higher order thinking processes

PBL can be a vehicle for providing students from all backgrounds with both the content and skills they need to achieve at high levels in their life. If you are feeling apprehension about your students' skills and their ability to do PBL, trust that this book will provide you with a step-by-step guide to scaffold meaningful learning for your students and that every one of your students is capable and deserving of such quality learning experiences. To learn more about making PBL accessible to all levels of students, check out the companion website (resources.corwin.com/keepitrealPBLsecondary).

Chapter 2
The Role of the Teacher in PBL

The Paradigm Shift

In its truest form, PBL (project-based learning) includes a teacher and a student working side by side. In academia, the phrase for this is *collegial pedagogy* and is best displayed in practice by the work of Lissa Soep at Youth Radio. Soep paints a picture of what you will find in an authentic PBL classroom—teachers learning alongside the student rather than delivering information in front of the student (2008). No longer is the teacher the "sage on the stage" because there is, in fact, great value in the power of equal.

The teacher is also viewed as an "activator" who is deeply engaged with students rather than as a mere "facilitator" of learning. Larmer (2016a), in agreement with Hattie's findings, argues this:

> For too long, constructivist-learning educators have romanticized the potential of independent student learning, using the inappropriate metaphor of "inquiry-based" or "discovery" learning. Good teachers . . . have never been limpid guides or stage-bound sages. Instead they are activators, bringing about changes in their students. (para. 13)

Instructional Best Practices

This shift in teaching and learning requires some changes in the classroom:

- Open-ended driving questions and project possibilities
- Voice and choice in topics of learning, final products, and project paths
- Nontraditional research methodologies to explore what is happening in real time
- The comfort and ability (and sometimes adventurous spirit) of the teacher to relinquish control and say, "I don't know, but let's find out"

Additionally, for PBL to be effective, Reagan (2015)—informed by Hattie's work—explains that the PBL teacher will need to be able to

- Scaffold background knowledge
- Facilitate meaningful student discussion

● **FIGURE 2.1** Jenny facilitating a "project audit" reflective exercise at Lake Elementary, Vista Unified School District, California

- Allow for risk-taking
- Build a culture around growth mindset
- Ask higher order questions
- Give effective feedback
- Direct inquiry and inferencing

PBL facilitators must also self-identify as being lifelong learners. An important element of this is modeling the growth mindset that we hope to see in our students. Another critical component of this mindset is acknowledging that those methods, courses, and teacher content exams we all took likely only provided preparation for a fraction of the content a PBL teacher facilitates in the learning process. If that gives you a little bit of anxiety, find some comfort in knowing that in PBL you aren't expected to have all the answers. The expectation is that you will again model what it means to be a learner and show your students how to go about finding the answers to the questions you *both* have. Yes, this means you will be reading more, watching YouTube videos on your mobile device at home, or queuing up a documentary on a Friday night. But you know what it also means? Your students will be doing the same because together you are learning about work that matters to them and the world around us, right now!

> *In PBL, you aren't expected to have all the answers.*

Adult Agency

Being a PBL facilitator requires a great deal of agency during the project planning and facilitation process. It is important to note that agency isn't just for our students; the term and way of being can and should be applied to adults as well. Throughout your PBL journey, you will be required to have a growth mindset, and you will need to be actively involved in your learning. Given this, how will you take control of your learning? How will you display ownership of your development as a PBL facilitator? How will you build relationships with colleagues, seek resources, and ask questions about your PBL learning?

Agency is defined by Hitlin and Elder (2007) by four overlapping concepts, two of which apply to being an adult learner in PBL:

1) Identity agency: What we believe about ourselves and the ways that we wish to be perceived by others.

2) Life-course agency: Actions that we take to affect future outcomes.

To learn more about the definition of *agency* and how it relates to PBL, visit the companion website (resources.corwin.com/keepitrealPBLsecondary).

And finally, part of being a lifelong learner is settling with the ugly truth (or beautiful truth, depending on how you look at it) that you will never "arrive." There is no ultimate destination in learning because our world continues to tilt and turn and we continue to evolve as humans. Given this, do your best to "trust the process" and "find comfort in the discomfort"—or at least get used to those mantras because you are going to hear them a lot from your PBL colleagues.

PBL Teacher Profile

Use Table 2.1 to help you further understand your role as a PBL facilitator. Oftentimes, teachers share that they aren't clear what PBL looks like in action. These teacher moves and phrases can help you process through what PBL may look like for *you*!

Find your tribe! Maybe teachers in your school aren't ready to try PBL, but guess what? There are a lot of teachers out there who are, so find them on social media. Look up the hashtags #hqpbl, #pblchat, and #shareyourlearning, to name just a few! Follow colleagues with these same interests.

NTKs referenced in Table 2.1 is short for need to knows, which is a process that starts during the project launch and is revisited every day to guide student-driven learning and teacher instruction. More on that in Chapter 10!

● **TABLE 2.1** A PBL Facilitator

The PBL facilitator is ...	The PBL facilitator does ...	The PBL facilitator says ...
Collaborative Plans with colleagues, even those from other content areas	Frequent assessments of student learning to provide ongoing feedback to students	"Our goal for learning today is . . . , which is related to the project's driving question . . ."
Reflective Seeks feedback on their work and ideas, strives to continue learning	Deliver/facilitate content in a variety of ways, such as running workshops, setting up labs, and maintaining traditional approaches when appropriate	"In the NTKs, you said you needed to learn x, so today we are going to learn about x by doing y."
In command of their content Is well versed in standards and engaging ways of teaching content	Active check-ins on learning and makes adjustments to remain responsive to student needs and interests	"I want my students to remember long term. . . .This content relates to the real-world by . . ."
A model of agency Displays a growth mindset	Communicate learning targets and plans/prepares in advance to facilitate learning tied to outcomes/targets	"On our project rubric, you are 'developing' in these ways . . . , and to become 'proficient' you need to . . ."
Solution-oriented Finds ways to creatively problem-solve PBL challenges that arise from large student caseloads at the secondary level	Build bridges between school and the community as well as school and home.	"I know in your XXXX class you are working on XXX, so we are going to support that by XXX."

Add your own ideas here! What does being a PBL facilitator mean to you? What shifts will you need to make? What will it look like in action—what will you say and do?

Chapter 3
Project Brainstorming

The brainstorming phase of project planning is the most fun! This is the chance to throw all your ideas on the wall without any worries. I like to tell teachers, "We aren't marrying these ideas; we are just dating them for now." There isn't any one right way to go about brainstorming—it's truly unique to every teacher and his or her style of ideation. Regardless of how you go about coming up with your project ideas, what follow are some pointers to help shape your ideas.

Where to Look for Ideas

Standards are typically presented conceptually or thematically. They give you a big idea of what you need to cover (e.g., law of motion, argumentative writing, geometric measurement and dimension). Consider the big ideas related to your standards and then generate a list of project ideas by asking, "How does this content relate to an issue in the community or the world?" Or "How does this relate to a concept or theme in my standards?" And most importantly, "Why should my students care about this content?"

Rather than starting with your standards and making a connection to the real world, you can also go in the reverse order. When I'm in project-brainstorming mode, it seems like everywhere I look I see project potential—the impact of car accidents when the driver is texting, access to healthy food options, development affecting a community or population, health and wellness issues, and so on. I always carry a journal with me so I can jot these ideas down while they are fresh. Look around your community—see what problems need to be solved and if you can make an authentic connection to your standards. Some examples to help get you started follow.

Problems in the Community ⟶ Content Standard Connections

Problems in the Community	Content Standard Connections
Safe driving	NGSS PS2-1, PS2-2, PS2-3
Global satellite development and use of its data	Science- NGSS HS-ETS1-1, HS-ETS1-4. HS-ESS3-6, MS-ESS3-5 HS-ESS3-4, HS-ESS3-1
Food and its journey from a scientific process in the field/farm to table	Science- NGSS LS2.B, LS4.D, ESS3.A
Sugar consumption in the USA today	ELA- W-2 a-f, W-4, W-5, W-6, W-7, W-8; SL-1, SL-4, SL-5 Science- NGSS-PS1-2
New playground or building design	Math- CCSS 8.G.B.6 Science- ETS1-2

Try it out! Write down some PBL ideas that come to mind as you think about issues in your community.

Standards ⟶ Real world	Real world ⟶ Standards

Collaborative Brainstorming

Two heads are always better than one, so I strongly encourage teachers to collaborate with colleagues when brainstorming ideas (see Figure 3.1). Here are a few of my favorite protocols for brainstorming project ideas (check the companion website for more):

- Fellow educator Brooke Tobia came up with the concept of a "Mindful Minute" exercise in which you mention your content topic and a partner rattles off related words and issues that come to mind. This can be a fun, creative exercise to do during a staff meeting.
- Check out the book *Gamestorming* (2010) by Dave Gray, Sunni Brown, and James Macanufo for fun ideas such as "Brain Writes" and "3–2–1," which help you hear from a variety of voices to draw upon diverse perspectives for the direction of your project.
- The "Wagon Wheel Protocol" from NSRF or the "Carousel Protocol" from Expeditionary Learning are great ways to capture a variety of ideas in a short amount of time.

Tip: **It may seem odd, but include colleagues from content areas other than your own—they will bring a diverse perspective and push your project thinking. This may even open the door for cross-collaboration between content areas!**

You can also engage students in the brainstorming process to allow for some "voice" in the project-planning process. Bring them into the process early on to ask them for initial ideas (similar to what you did with your colleagues), or you can involve them in a project-tuning protocol as a "Critical Friend" once your ideas are more formulated. Visit the companion website to learn more about "Critical Friends."

Photo courtesy of Chris Nelson Photography.

● **FIGURE 3.1** Jenny and a group of teachers at Lake Elementary providing feedback on fellow colleagues' project plans

Group Brainstorming Best Practices

- **Wild ideas are always welcome!**
- **Make all ideas visible. Write them down and don't erase them!**
- **Give yourself a lot of space—either a big whiteboard or a large roll of butcher paper.**
- **Use the language of improv: "Yes . . . and . . ."**

Still feeling stuck on where to get started? Here is a bank of ideas that may give you some direction:

Grade	Content	Real-World Connection
6th grade	NGSS (life science), math (data), ELA (informational text)	Human impact in our local ecosystem; beach/lagoon water use in protected areas and parks
7th grade	NGSS, Health/PE, ELA	Plan and defense for best use of local development
8th grade	The Great Reform	Social issues that arguably need reform today—local to global issues
9th grade	Math (statistics), ELA	Collecting and analyzing data on local issues; informing others or using data to develop argument
10th grade	French Revolution	Recipe for revolutions; change-agents today, domestic and/or international
11th grade	American democratic ideals, ELA (narratives)	Connections to human experiences through leadership, political, economic, and social issues of today
12th grade	ELA (argumentative writing)	Develop and defend a position on a contemporary issue, rooted in a historic or scientific issue

Once you have an idea that you like, you can continue to give your brainstorm some shape by thinking through this flow.

The PBL Brainstorming Planning Form is designed to capture your wild and crazy ideas. This is not the place to get married to any particular idea; it is simply a place to organize your thoughts and start to make some connections. If you come up with a big idea but can't connect it to any standard you need to cover, scratch that idea and start with a new line of thinking.

PBL Brainstorming Planning Form

Big ideas

These topics should be related to content areas for your grade level.

Early humans, ancient civilizations

Argumentative writing

Narrative writing

Real-world context

How does this relate to an authentic problem that is relevant to your community/students?

Many social issues in San Francisco: homelessness, population density, poverty, affordability (re: cost of living)

Standards and skills

What standards can you see connecting to your idea?

Social studies (CA) 6.1: Students describe what is known through archaeological studies of the early physical and cultural development of humankind from the Paleolithic era to the agricultural revolution.

CCSS.ELA-LITERACY.W.6.1

Write arguments to support claims with clear reasons and relevant evidence.

ELA (CCSS) CCSS.ELA-LITERACY.W.6.3

Write narratives to develop real or imagined experiences or events using effective technique, relevant descriptive details, and well-structured event sequences.

Final product

What can students create/do/share?

Letter to local official

Potential real-world connection

Who might you bring in? Where might you take students out?

Community location visits for observation/ interviews

Urban planner, local nonprofit or community agency

Source: © 2018 Jennifer Pieratt.

Download a blank version of this template at resources.corwin.com/keepitrealPBLsecondary

Chapter 4
Planning PBL for Your Year

●**FIGURE 4.1** Jenny working with a Lake Elementary teacher on upcoming project plans

Big Picture and Big Ideas

Deciding where to begin with planning your first project can be overwhelming. The process I will walk you through in this chapter is designed to help you identify the "easiest lift"—meaning, the sweet spot where content connections feel natural and you will be set up with a strong foundation for a quality project. To do that, you will consider your year at a glance, identify the enduring understanding, consider time commitments, and focus on *one* area in which you feel really good about diving into PBL!

Power and Driving Standards

The early steps of the project-planning process require that we stay in "big-picture mode." What this means is that you will need to zoom way back to look at your year, as a whole. Start by defining the major themes or big ideas for your year, as they relate to your power standards.

Ainsworth (2014) defines *power standards* as those that are essential rather than nice to know. Power standards possess the following criteria:

- Long-term value (i.e., endurance)
- Leverage (i.e., it will be of value to multiple disciplines)
- Readiness for the next level of learning (i.e., they are essential skills needed for the following grade level or next level of instruction)

Tip: Your power standards are typically the standards language in bold or listed as the section heading on your curriculum documents.

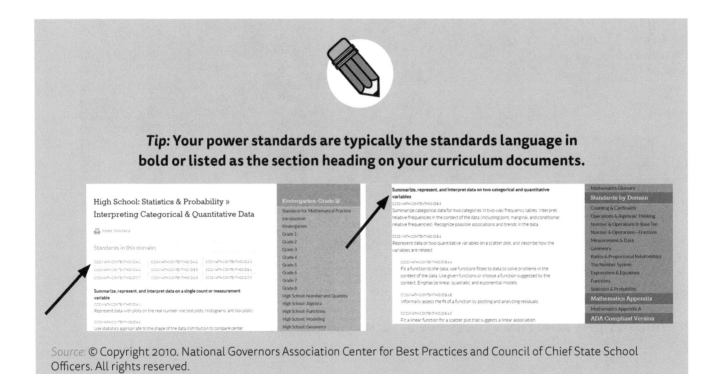

Within these power standards, I often focus on science and social studies, which I refer to as "driving standards." For example, Lake Washington School District provides its teachers with power standards for all content areas: arts, health, literacy, mathematics, science, social studies, and technology. This is a lot of information to look at all at once when thinking about PBL, so narrow in on just the power standards for science and social studies—those are your "driving standards" for project design.

Both science and social studies standards are presented thematically and more readily provide context for a project, which ELA or math can easily support. For example, "human impact on local ecosystems," for science, provides a nice big idea that a variety of informational reading and writing can support. Another example, for social studies, could be "citizenship in a democracy," which serves as another big idea, which math could support through data collection and analysis.

Rooted in your power standards, use the form provided to identify the big ideas you will cover in a year for your driving standards (in science, math, social studies, and ELA). Table 4.1 provides an example of several power standards and the thematic big ideas behind them, and Table 4.2 is a blank template for you to fill in with your own power standards and big ideas!

● **TABLE 4.1** Determining Big Ideas From Driving Standards

Standards	Big Ideas
MS-PS3-3 Energy Apply scientific principles to design, construct, and test a device that either minimizes or maximizes thermal energy transfer.	Thermal energy transfer
CA SS 8.2 Students analyze the political principles underlying the U.S. Constitution and compare the enumerated and implied powers of the federal government.	Laws and government in the U.S. past to present
NGSS HS-PS2-3 Motion and Stability: Forces and Interactions Apply scientific and engineering ideas to design, evaluate, and refine a device that minimizes the force on a macroscopic object during a collision.	Force, motion, impact
CCSS.ELA-LITERACY.W.9-10.2 A-F Write informative/explanatory texts to examine and convey complex ideas, concepts, and information clearly and accurately through the effective selection, organization, and analysis of content.	Informational writing
CCSS.ELA-LITERACY.RI.11-12.9 Analyze seventeenth, eighteenth, and nineteenth century foundational U.S. documents of historical and literary significance (including the Declaration of Independence, the Preamble to the Constitution, the Bill of Rights, and Lincoln's Second Inaugural Address) for their themes, purposes, and rhetorical features.	Analyze U.S. historical documents
CCSS.MATH.CONTENT.6.SP.B.4 Display numerical data in plots on a number line, including dot plots, histograms, and box plots.	Distributions
CA SS 11.1 Students analyze the significant events in the founding of the nation and its attempts to realize the philosophy of government described in the Declaration of Independence.	Rights of man, human nature, role of government

Source: Science Standards from NGSS Lead States. 2013. Next Generation Science Standards: For States, By States. Washington, DC: The National Academies Press. California Social Studies Standards from © 2000 California Department of Education. ELA and Math Standards from © Copyright 2010. National Governors Association Center for Best Practices and Council of Chief State School Officers. All rights reserved.

● **TABLE 4.2** Determining Big Ideas From Driving Standards—Your Turn

Standards	Big Ideas

Make Content Connections: Planning Interdisciplinary Projects

A note about interdisciplinary planning: When two teachers from two different content areas are collaborating on a project, I encourage the social studies or science teacher to "drive" the project-planning process. Both social studies and science serve as a great context for a project, which math, ELA (English language arts), or VAPA (visual and performing arts) can easily support (see Figure 4.2).

Driving standards are those that lead the project planning because they more easily provide a context for project learning. Typically, driving standards surround social studies/history or science.

After both teachers have completed Table 4.2, you can review these documents together. Look to see if you can make any connections between the big ideas across these two disciplines. For example, in Table 4.3 you can see what interdisciplinary project planning looks like in action for eighth or 11th grade. In the first row, social studies/history started out as a driving standard, and ELA made a content connection to those historical documents through reading primary sources.

● **TABLE 4.3 Sample Cross-Content Connection Brainstorm**

Driving Standard Big Idea	Cross-Content Connections
Social studies: Analyze U.S. historical documents	ELA: Reading primary (historical) sources
Science: Force, motion	ELA: Short research reading, informational writing
Social studies: Westward expansion	Math: Statistics related to two populations ELA: Narrative reading and writing
Engineering: Design for social need	ELA: Informational writing, persuasive writing Math: Data and measurement
Science: Matter, interactions	ELA: Informational writing

While it's OK in this big-picture brainstorming phase to make loose connections, you will want to be careful to avoid setting yourself up for a thematic unit (activities connected by the same topic/theme, such as "animals," "community," "space and planets") or a dessert project rather than true, integrated PBL in which all learning happens in service of the project. For example, a science teacher may want her or his students to complete a project on water consumption and

● **FIGURE 4.2** A Reality Road Map for Project Planning

A Reality RoadMap for
Brainstorming Project Ideas

Another #realtalk PBL Resource with Jenny

IS THERE RIGOR AT THE CORE?

Is your project idea grounded in your standards? Will this project idea lead to Deeper Learning?

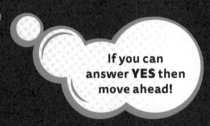

If you can answer **YES** then move ahead!

IS THERE POTENTIAL FOR ENDURING UNDERSTANDING?

Will your students remember this stuff 10 years from now? Does it transfer to other contexts? Can you easily tell me why students should care about this content/project?

ARE THERE REAL-WORLD CONNECTIONS?

Does this topic relate to an authentic problem or issue in your local community? Or perhaps the global community (for older students)?

If you answer **NO** then **STOP!**

IS THERE ENOUGH JUICE FOR THE SQUEEZE?

Will students gain more by learning this through the completion/process of a final product? Or can this content be learned quickly and doesn't offer any benefit to elongating this specific content through a project? Is it worth the time?!

IS THERE AN AUDIENCE?

If you have gotten this far, then you are likely to have an authentic idea ... are there people outside of your school who will benefit from students sharing their learning? ... beyond parents!

conservation, and the ELA teacher says, "We can read a fictional story about water." While these are thematically related because they both have to do with water, a fictional account does not necessarily inform a better scientific understanding of the content required for the project.

Integrated projects are those that have a similar broad theme across content areas (e.g., water, relationships, cause/effect, etc.). Interdisciplinary projects truly use multiple content areas to enhance the completion of a project and equally depend on an understanding of all content areas involved in order to complete the project.

An example of an interdisciplinary project would be if a social studies teacher wants students to use what they know about history to analyze a current social issue. Students will then survey and analyze statistical responses in math and use that data as part of an argumentative writing piece (in ELA) to produce a digital PSA, which will be assessed for all three content areas.

Moving through the project design process, the following would be possible red flags for an integrated project rather than an interdisciplinary project:

- Reading about fictional characters (say, an animal) in ELA that do not directly tie back to learning that is necessary for the final product in a science project on the environment (more on this in Chapter 5!). While this is thematically related because it is about ecosystems, it does not inform student learning related to the completion of their project/final product on unity and diversity (per NGSS DCI).

- Art projects, perhaps on a profile of a change agent in U.S. history, that do not directly relate to historical or literary content covered in a social studies or ELA class. Again, while a teacher may be able to loosely connect these products, they fall under the umbrella of American leaders; without a direct correlation to the standards or tie to the final product, it stands as a dessert project (if done at the end of the unit) or a thematic (integrated) activity *somewhat* related to a project or unit.

- Incorporation of mathematical statistics when it does not inform the larger project or final product. Yes, students can collect and analyze statistics on almost anything; however, if it is not integrated into a final product (say, as data to support a claim), then you have hit a dead end for an interdisciplinary project connection; save this idea for a PrBL (problem-based learning) unit later.

#realtalk: A project done completely at home that is focused on arts and crafts without visible content or skill mastery or that is done at the end of a unit of learning is not PBL—it's a "dessert project."

To further help you with this process, you can use Ainsworth's (2014) trick: Ask yourself if it is "essential" that students know about the one content area to complete the other content area. Or would it simply be "nice for them to know" about the two content areas, and they can exist independently of one another?

If at any point you are unable to answer these questions, then stop! Abort mission!

Identify a *Real* Connection

The bedrock to authenticity in project design is ensuring that there is a real-world connection and relevance to your students (see Table 4.4). To help you with this, here are two important questions to ask yourself when you are considering if your content areas are a natural fit for designing a project:

1. How does this relate to an important issue in the community? (local or global)
2. Why do my students need to learn about this? Why will/ should they care?

● **TABLE 4.4** Making Community Connections to Content

Driving Standard Big Idea	Community Connection
Social studies: Analyze U.S. historical documents	Local, current civil rights/government issues
Science: Force, motion	Driver, pedestrian safety at school
Social studies: Westward expansion	Compare/contrast with current stories of immigration from the news
Engineering: Design for social need	New school, housing development design
Science: Matter, interactions	Composting, recycling

As you look at your big content ideas and maybe even cross-content connections, what real-world issues jump out to you? Write them down here!

Pacing Your Project

The next step is to start thinking about general pacing and timing for your project (see Table 4.5). This step of the planning requires that teachers have some autonomy to move content around a bit in your year; if you are on a strict pacing guide from your district, this will be difficult to complete in a way that feels authentic to your project plans. Assuming that you have some curricular flexibility, begin by creating some space holders for your existing units and potential project plans.

If you are looking for scope and sequence documents for math, emergentmath.com has you covered for grades K–12. Visit the companion website (resources.corwin.com/ keepitrealPBLsecondary) for links to fully completed pacing guides for math. *Note:* While these are aligned to a PrBL framework, it can easily be a starting point that is built out for PBL. You will also find a detailed scope and sequence for a ninth-grade integrated science class in Appendix A.

● **TABLE 4.5** Pacing Guide for Project Planning

Big Ideas	September	October	November	December	January

Is There Enough Juice for the Squeeze?

Before we go any further, let's look at the initial timing you have allocated. Does it make sense for your project idea to be the vehicle for teaching a specific content area or skill? Or is it simply additional practice or a review of something previously covered? Depending on how you answer, that will determine your pacing and time devoted to the project.

This is an important reality check for you. Teachers often share that PBL feels like it takes too much time and doesn't allow them to cover all of their content and related skills. It's true—PBL does celebrate "depth not breadth" with content coverage; however, if you aren't being asked to do "wall-to-wall PBL," then you have some options here. Covering a small substandard (not a power standard) should not take four to six weeks; so if you have allocated a unit to stretch to align with a driver standard for a project, know that either (1) it's not the right fit for this project and that content should simply be covered as a smaller problem-based unit separate from the project; or (2) the smaller standards will be covered in the project, but separate time during the day will also be allocated to additional content and skills (more on daily management and scheduling in Chapter 8!).

While you may have a few ideas up to this point, as we move forward in the project design process just pick one to build out for your first time. Identify which of your curricular connections you are most interested in pursuing for a project with your students and the one that feels like the easiest lift—make sure it has an authentic real-world connection that you think would excite your kids and the pacing works within your year—and let's go!

Still not sure where to get started? Check out *Project Based Teaching* (2018) by Suzie Boss and John Larmer for a great exercise on how to align standards to your project ideas.

Chapter 5
Planning With the End in Mind

To plan our project, we will go through a process that is deeply inspired by backward design (Wiggins & McTighe, 2012), which you might remember from your teacher credentialing program. Think about the end you have in mind: What content and skills do you want students to master? Let's come up with the road map to get them there through intentional statements, questions, and final products!

Drafting Enduring Understanding

Your enduring understanding (EU) is a simple teacher-facing statement that serves as the "umbrella" or big idea for planning; it is rooted in your standards. Writing your EU helps you get clear on what you want students to remember 10 years from now. When they have left you and are in college or their career, what do you hope they look back on and remember learning in your classroom?

Photo courtesy of Chris Nelson Photography.

● **FIGURE 5.1** Jenny and Lake Elementary teachers searching student work for tenants of high-quality PBL

Your EU is general and should transcend context—that is, it should be applicable to what students are learning right now, but could also apply to any other time, situation, or place later in their future. EUs also easily transfer across content areas if you are planning an interdisciplinary project.

Your EU also helps you address a best practice of PBL design—authenticity. Authenticity is a synonym for *real-world connection*; in other words, what is an authentic way for students to learn content and skills? For example, how would a scientist authentically research or solve a problem? How would a local politician go about proposing a change for the community? What is a connection between the content and the local or global community? What makes the content *real*? Creating an authentic EU is the foundation for creating an engaging project (see Table 5.1).

● **TABLE 5.1** Sample EU Statements

- The probability of an event can be used to predict the probability of future events.

- The principles and ideals underlying American democracy are designed to promote the freedom of the American people.

- There are scientific theories that can inform the choices we make behind the wheel.

- People have displayed resilience in the face of challenges, and we can learn from them when we too struggle.

- Humans impact the environment, and we can make local changes that can lead to global changes.

- There is value to understanding historical pillars of civilization as we innovate the future.

- Our words and numbers have value in persuading people to act.

Example

Project Planner

Title: **"The Human Experience: Past to Present"**   Grade: **6**

Content Area: **Humanities**

Enduring Understanding:

As humans, we adapt to our surroundings, and there are parallels between how early man responded to life and the ways in which people in our community respond to life.

Standards and Skills:

Social Studies (CA) 6.1 Students describe what is known through archaeological studies of the early physical and cultural development of humankind from the Paleolithic era to the agricultural revolution.

Crafting Driving Questions

A driving question (DQ) is the big question that guides student learning throughout the course of the project. The DQ is student-facing and helps address the daily question "Why are we learning this?" The DQ also helps make a connection between what students are learning and your EU because the two are directly related.

What you want students to produce or create at the end of the project will inform what kind of driving question you craft. Your DQ should directly relate to your final product (up next in Chapter 6!). According to Tony Vincent (2014), there are five types of driving questions. For example, you might want your project to do one or more of the following:

1. **Solve a problem:** There's a real-world predicament with multiple solutions.

    - How can we stop phantom traffic jams?

2. **Be educational:** The purpose of the project is to teach others.

    - How can we teach our neighbors about the potential impacts of proposed development plans?

3. **Convince others:** Students persuade a specific audience to do something.

    - How can we convince our school board to fund an updated and safe student parking lot?

4. **Have a broad theme:** It tackles big ideas.

    - How does conflict lead to change?

5. **Be divergent:** Make predictions about alternative timelines and scenarios.

    - What if World War I never happened?

Here are a few examples of driving questions:

- What is the recipe for a revolution? (8th-grade/10th-grade social studies, 12th-grade government)
- How can satellites be leveraged to promote a more just planet? (9th-grade/10th-grade integrated science)
- How does electromagnetism play a role in how sharks and humans interact, and how does this interaction affect their relationship and ecology? (9th-grade integrated science)
- To what extent is DNA destiny? (10th-grade integrated science)
- To what extent is U.S. history a history of progress? (11th-grade social studies, 12th-grade government)
- Who is entitled to own what? (12th-grade government)
- How can we use our knowledge of entrepreneurism to do good for our community? (12th-grade English for business)

What is the difference between an essential question and a driving question?

Essential questions are used to engage learners in thoughtful "meaning making" to help them develop and deepen their understanding of important ideas and processes that support such transfer (McTighe & Wiggins, 2012). A project could have a number of smaller essential questions if that is part of your existing practice. A driving question, however, is the larger question that drives all student learning within the project. Think of the DQ as the big umbrella and smaller essential questions can come under it within individual lessons or phases of the project.

Tip: **When writing your driving question, start with the words** *how,* *why, or what if.*

To craft your driving question, come back to your EU and ground your question here so that all student learning that is happening in the project is in service of your DQ and rooted in your EU (see Table 5.2). You want your driving question to be open-ended—students should not be able to easily answer it with a yes or a no or give a simple list. Think of a problem, challenge, or solution that students can't easily ask Siri or Alexa or type into Google. You also want to consider questions that will allow students to grow in their response—how they answer this question on Day 1 of the project should be different from Day 5 and Day 15.

● **TABLE 5.2** Sixth-Grade Project Plans, Focusing on Driving Question

Driving Question:

What is the human experience of adapting to life? How are the current challenges of those living in San Francisco similar and different to those faced by early man?

Final Products

When thinking about a final product for your project, consider the project's outcome—what will students ultimately create, make, perform, or do? What will be the final, tangible product at the end of the project?

Again, go back to your end. Think about a final product that will showcase content mastery and twenty-first century skill development that you have identified for this project. The Final Product Idea Bank box lists some of my favorites, and you can also see Figures 5.2 and 5.3.

Final Product Idea Bank

- Letter to government official
- Informational brochure for local organization
- Public blog post response
- Infographic for public use
- Narrative writing in a published compilation
- Awareness campaign (PSA)
- Social media campaign
- Business Fakebook page
- Instagram chat book
- Panel timeline exhibit for local museum
- Recruitment poster
- Panel discussion simulation
- Political platform slogan and speech
- Memorial design, dedication ceremony
- Documentary

- Design and conduct a survey
- Design and conduct a focus group
- Traveling school exhibit
- Collaborative wiki
- Class website
- Photo essays for public display
- Community mural and peace table
- Digital PSA
- Legal policy brief
- School culture or design proposal
- Found poetry, art installation
- Two-voice poetry recording
- Digital scrapbook
- Digital diorama
- Stop-motion film
- Flipbook

●FIGURE 5.2 A sample final product for a sixth-grade infographic project, completed on Piktochart, to compile student research and calculated data on sugar consumption in America. For more information on student-created infographics, visit the companion website (resources.corwin.com/keepitrealPBLsecondary).

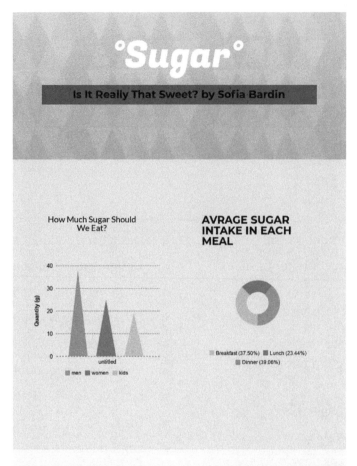

● **FIGURE 5.3** A sample final product for a high school digital media arts class. Students were assigned to pick a spot they loved and conduct a formal portrait session that incorporated photography concepts and photo editing covered in class.

For more final products for all grade levels, you can visit High Tech High's website (www .hightechhigh.org) under "Student Work" or visit the companion website (resources.corwin.com/ keepitrealPBLsecondary).

Voice and Choice

If you are a superstar and hoping to provide voice and choice for your students' final products in your first project, that is awesome! I encourage you to limit your students' options the first time you do PBL to keep it manageable (both in scaffolding and assessing). Consider offering three different final products for students to pick from, all of which showcase the same content and skills. Or perhaps the whole class will do the same final product, but each student has choice in the content or how to access the content.

#realtalk: Voice and choice does not mean total student control over all things—that can lead to anarchy! Some structure is OK to ensure that students will master the content and skills needed for assessment.

A Note About Differentiation

When you are thinking about the—say, three—final product options you are going to give students, you can think about them as what would be accessible to a "high," "medium," or "low" student. Or you can think about providing final product options that align with a variety of intelligences. Oftentimes, you may have one or two students that supersede their peers when it comes to project work. In this case, you can provide a "challenge option," or for older students, you can invite "challenge proposals." A challenge proposal can be a basic template completed by the student that includes the following steps:

1. Their alternate final product and links to any inspiration or models
2. How their proposal explicitly addresses the project driving question
3. What steps they will need to take to complete this (*hint:* this is simply a modification of the existing project benchmarks)

4. A modified project calendar if needed (you can work together on this)
5. Resources you both identify as additional supports for them
6. A signed agreement among student, teacher, and parent for completing all of the previous steps by the same due date as their peers

Final Product:

Photo Essay, Letter to local representative

Culminating Experience

Since you have an authentic idea planned, there is likely a natural fit for a real audience who would benefit from interacting with your students' work. Think beyond the walls of your school—who needs to be inspired or informed by your students' learning, and how can you share your students' work with them? The Culminating Experience Idea Bank has some ideas to consider, and you can also see Table 5.3.

Need more help thinking through how to share student work at the end of your project? Check out shareyourlearning.org for exhibition resources.

● **TABLE 5.3** **Culminating Experience Idea Bank**

- Community performance
- Community exhibition
- Evening with the arts (in a local studio or community organization)
- Schoolwide exhibition
- Book-signing party
- Shark tank pitch
- Red-carpet screening
- Submission to local newspaper with press release
- "Reveal"/ribbon-cutting ceremony

Culminating Experience:

Display of photo essays in a central, community location (e.g., public library or city hall)

Now is a great "pause point" to seek out collegial feedback on your project ideas before moving forward. Check the companion website for a variety of simple protocols you can use for this process, or try using CraftED's "Thought Push Protocol" found in the following box. We will reference a more in-depth tuning protocol later in this book, but for now, it's good to share your ideas and be sure you are on the right track before moving too far down the road.

Thought Push Protocol

1. Presenter shares project overview. (3 min.)

2. Presenter removes him- or herself from circle.

3. Circle discusses the following:

   I like . . . (2 min.)

   I love . . . (2 min.)

   I'm thinking about . . . (2 min.)

4. Presenter reflects. (1 min.)

*Note: This protocol is a modified combination of several tuning protocols from New Tech Network, National School Reform Faculty, PBLWorks, and *The Power of Protocols* (2003) by Joseph McDonald.

Chapter 6
Benchmarking Your Project

FIGURE 6.1 Jenny and Lake Elementary teachers conduct a project reflective exercise

What Is Benchmarking?

Benchmarking in project-based learning is really just about building in project milestones. It involves thinking about your end in mind (final product, content, and skills) and how you can break it down into digestible learning chunks, both for you and your students.

Typically, there are anywhere from four to six benchmarks in a project. Again, these are just phases you can move through that will serve as catch points for you to make sure students have mastered content and skills prior to moving forward. You can scaffold, differentiate, and reteach as needed in between the benchmarks.

Here is a sample of how benchmarks flow with your instruction in a project:

> Benchmark #1: Background knowledge ➤ Scaffolding, instruction, differentiation
>
> Benchmark #2: Problem-solving, field work ➤ Scaffolding, instruction, differentiation
>
> Benchmark #3: Final product development, Phase I draft ➤ Scaffolding, instruction, differentiation
>
> Benchmark #4: Final product, process refinement ➤ Scaffolding, instruction, differentiation

Related to the power standards, Ainsworth's (2014) discussion cites the work of Douglas Reeves, who has coined a term known as the *safety-net curriculum*, which is "a very limited set of learning objectives organized for each grade and for each subject. It is not the total curriculum—just the 'safety net' that every teacher should ensure that every student knows" (p. 111).

You can think about your project benchmarks as the safety net for your curriculum. For example, think about the ELA power standard CCSS.ELA-LITERACY.W.9-10.3: "Write narratives to develop real or imagined experiences or events using effective technique, well-chosen details, and well-structured event sequences." The following would be possible benchmarks within a project that would serve as safety nets to ensure that students mastered the content and skills they needed for 9th- and 10th-grade ELA:

> Benchmark 1: Reading and analyzing narratives—focusing on point of view
>
> Benchmark 2: Narrative techniques—literary devices/figurative language

Benchmark 3: Storyboard—drafting of narrative story

Benchmark 4: Revisions—reflection and final draft of narrative story

As a humanities teacher, the importance of designing and implementing thoughtful benchmarks in the writing process is crucial. Every project that has writing as a centerpiece has to be designed with benchmarks that create opportunities for every student to learn. I actively try to design and implement benchmarks for our writing in projects that break down every element of formatting, style, and expression. It is great to see how effective benchmarks in writing empower students to write at their best.

—Asal Meyer, 12th-grade literature teacher at High Tech High North County

Identifying Deliverables

Each benchmark is tied to a deliverable—something concrete that the student turns in for formative assessment and feedback. Yes, smaller daily checks for understanding are happening—say, when students turn in worksheets, journal entries, labs, or through class discussions—but you will formally (formatively) assess at each benchmark using rows from the rubric you will design in the next chapter. These deliverables are critical because they allow you the opportunity to provide feedback to students, while also affording students the opportunity to address the feedback before moving forward in the project. This is critical to rigorous, quality PBL because it ensures that students are learning the content and skills for their grade level—hence, the "safety net" discussed earlier. Later in the chapter, you can see a sixth-grade humanities example, but Appendix A also provides sixth-grade science, ninth-grade humanities, and 12th-grade entrepreneurism class samples if you want to see more.

#realtalk: You may notice that some of these deliverables are "traditional" in nature. Hopefully, this lets you breathe a sigh of relief—a lot of what you previously taught still applies!

Common Types of Project Deliverables for Formative Assessment

- Research documentation
- Storyboards or scripts
- Detailed artists' statements
- Critiques and revised drafts
- Detailed outlines, diagrams, or sketches
- Lab reports
- Quizzes

A Note About Differentiation

If you are teaching in a "full inclusion" school setting, a best practice is to partner up with your special education (SPED) teacher at this point in the planning process. Once you have identified your project benchmarks and deliverables, your SPED teacher will be able to easily identify which students are going to need additional supports to successfully complete these. Once this has been identified, you can work together (maybe even coteach!) to provide additional scaffolds as necessary. In PBL, the product is the same for every child; how we get them there may differ. If you want to dive into this more, check out Chapter 6 of Boss and Larmer's (2018) book *Project Based Teaching* and follow the incredible work of inclusion PBL teacher Kristen Uliasz (@MsUliasz) on Twitter.

> *In PBL, the product is the same for every child; how we get them there may differ.*

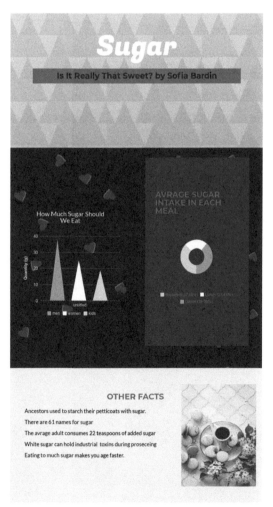

● FIGURE 6.2 Sample Project Infographic Benchmark

An infographic can be used as an early benchmark deliverable for the background research phase of a project, or it can be used as a final product for any grade level. If used for a final product, a draft of the infographic would be the final benchmark prior to completing the end product of a published and perfected infographic to put on display. Figure 6.2 shows the first draft of an infographic on a sixth-grade research project on U.S. sugar consumption. Notice that this draft is missing key information. The students conducted a self-reflection, received peer feedback and expert feedback, and then revised their work— you saw the final product in the previous chapter. Figure 6.3 shows an infographic as a final product for the sixth-grade math and ELA project on sugar consumption that was posted at school during the week before Valentine's Day; however, this same final product was also just used by a high school physics teacher on a project about motion, force, and impact. Students applied content knowledge to create infographics on driver safety that were printed on poster-sized paper, framed, and mounted around the school for National Teen Driver Safety Week.

If you are looking to integrate technology into your project, try a few of my favorite apps and programs:

- Explain Everything is excellent for scientifically labeled diagrams, which can serve as a great deliverable.
- ThingLink can be fun for social studies and ELA as a way to capture a photo and put voice and text explanations within the photo, using a "hover over" feature.
- Piktochart infographics serve as a nice way to distill research and even data collection (numbers, charts, stats) into a visual that can be printed and easily displayed. I have seen this used as both a deliverable and a final product.
- Imovie and Paper Slides can be a fun alternative to traditional PowerPoint presentations.
- Garage Band recordings for 2 Voice Poetry can be used as both a deliverable or a final product.

"Teacher Tech Tools" is a website created for teachers by a teacher, Camille Nunnenkamp, to feel both comfortable and inspired to leverage technology in their classrooms. Teacher Tech Tools houses grade-level specific sample projects in which technology is used to assess students' evaluation and creation skills within a project. Each project example includes a step-by-step tutorial of the application or technological platform used for easy implementation in your classroom. To learn more, visit the companion website (resources.corwin .com/keepitrealPBLsecondary).

● FIGURE 6.3 Sample Project Final Product Infographic

Example

Benchmark Phases:

Benchmark #1: Early Humans

- Come back to NTKs as driver for lessons during this benchmark phase.

- Teacher will cover the topics as outlined in CA standards 6.1.1-3 through engaging activities of his or her choosing in addition to daily checks for understanding.

- Teacher will assign students to the following scaffold assignment to help them consider the life of one early human during the time periods discussed in this benchmark. Teacher will collect and check for understanding of content.

- Teacher will ask students to consider their Bio Sketch as they think about what a firsthand account/narrative for this person may have sounded like. What feelings might he or she have had about daily life?

- Teacher will provide lessons on narrative writing techniques as outlined in CCSS to help students explain the feelings and experiences of early man.

Benchmark #2: Compare/Contrast Past to Present

- Come back to NTKs as driver for lessons during this benchmark phase.

- Teacher will collect local news stories through a variety of mediums. Teacher will then facilitate a jigsaw lesson for students to learn about local issues in the community. Lesson will conclude with a class discussion or Socratic Seminar on key themes/issues in the community.

- Teacher will prepare students to go on a walking field trip to address the DQs: *What social issues are present in our local community? What do we see? What can we infer?*

- Teacher will debrief field work experience.

Student Deliverables:

1. Early Human Narrative

2. Voice Poetry

- Teacher will ask students to consider this:
  How is what we have learned about local community issues similar and different from issues that early humans faced?

Benchmark #3: Community Issues

3. Infographic

- Come back to NTKs as driver for lessons during this benchmark phase.

- Teacher will assign students to begin group research on identified topic (community issue) of choice.

- Teacher may decide to use the field work as a focus for the Question Formulation Technique for students to develop group driving questions for future research on local issues. Teacher should be sure to review source credibility, bias, and proper citations.

- Teacher may decide to bring in experts to discuss local issues as a form of field work.

- Teacher will provide a workshop on how to create an infographic as a way to distill group research into the most engaging and simplest format.

Benchmark #4: Human Stories/Experiences Related to Community Issues

4. Photo Essay

- Prior to the beginning of this benchmark phase, the teacher will want to identify a location for curating completed student photo essays.

- Come back to NTKs as driver for lessons during this benchmark phase.

- Teacher will introduce students to the concept of photo essays and analyze models using an Artful Thinking Routine.

- Teacher will provide a tech tutorial on how to edit photographs taken during previous field work.

- Teacher will provide a workshop on how to create a photo essay.

(Continued)

(Continued)

- Teacher may decide to have students complete a writing assignment to accompany photographs that includes narratives, subtitles, or informational writing.
- Teacher will ask students to come back to the project DQ as the prompt for developing a photo essay.

Benchmark #5: Civic Engagement

5. Letter to a Representative

- Come back to NTKs as driver for lessons during this benchmark phase.
- Teacher may choose to cover citizenship and democracy in Greece through engaging history lessons.
- Teacher will discuss the power of our voice and our role as citizens in a democracy. Teacher will help students identify an appropriate government representative or organization recipient for a letter they will be writing to persuade them to take action on a local community issue they have studied.
- Teacher will facilitate a writing workshop on how to write formal letters with a strong claim and reasoning.
- Teacher will take students through the entire writing process.

Complete the top of this form (EU, standards/skills, DQ, final product, culminating experience) to figure out how to organize the building blocks of your project.

Project Planner

Title: **"The Human Experience: Past to Present"**   Grade: **6**

Content Area: **Humanities**

Enduring Understanding:

As humans, we adapt to our surroundings, and there are parallels between how early humans responded to life and the ways in which people in our community respond to life.

Standards and Skills:

Social Studies (CA) 6.1 Students describe what is known through archaeological studies of the early physical and cultural development of humankind from the Paleolithic era to the agricultural revolution.

6.1.1 Describe the hunter-gatherer societies, including the development of tools and the use of fire.

6.1.2 Identify the locations of human communities that populated the major regions of the world and describe how humans adapted to a variety of environments.

6.1.3 Discuss the climatic changes and human modifications of the physical environment that gave rise to the domestication of plants and animals and new sources of clothing and shelter.

CCSS.ELA-LITERACY.W.6.1 A-E

Write arguments to support claims with clear reasons and relevant evidence.

ELA (CCSS) CCSS.ELA-LITERACY.W.6.3

Write narratives to develop real or imagined experiences or events using effective technique, relevant descriptive details, and well-structured event sequences.

- Oral communication: Use of digital media/visual displays
- Collaboration: Commitment to shared success
- Agency: Impact self and community; use effort and practice to grow
- Written communication: Development, organization, language, and conventions

(Continued)

(Continued)

Driving Question:

What is the human experience of adapting to life? How are the current challenges of those living in San Francisco similar and different to those faced by early man?

Final Product:

Photo essay; letter to local representative

Culminating Experience: **Display of photo essays in a central community location (e.g., public library or city hall)**

Benchmark Phases:

Benchmark #1: Early Humans

- Come back to NTKs as driver for lessons during this benchmark phase.

- Teacher will cover the topics as outlined in CA standards 6.1.1-3 through engaging activities of his or her choosing in addition to daily checks for understanding.

- Teacher will assign students to the following scaffold assignment to help them consider the life of one early human during the time periods discussed in this benchmark. Teacher will collect and check for understanding of content.

- Teacher will ask students to consider their Bio Sketch as they think about what a firsthand account/narrative for this person may have sounded like. What feelings might he or she have had about daily life?

- Teacher will provide lessons on narrative writing techniques as outlined in CCSS to help students explain the feelings and experiences of early man.

Student Deliverables:

1. Early Human Narrative

Benchmark #2: Compare/Contrast Past to Present

- Come back to NTKs as driver for lessons during this benchmark phase.

- Teacher will collect local news stories through a variety of mediums. Teacher will then facilitate a jigsaw lesson for students to learn about local issues in the community. Lesson will conclude with a class discussion or Socratic Seminar on key themes/issues in the community.

- Teacher will prepare students to go on a walking field trip to address the DQs: *What social issues are present in our local community? What do we see? What can we infer?*

- Teacher will debrief field work experience.

- Teacher will ask students to consider this: *How is what we have learned about local community issues similar and different from issues that early humans faced?*

Benchmark #3: Community Issues

- Come back to NTKs as driver for lessons during this benchmark phase.

- Teacher will assign students to begin group research on identified topic (community issue) of choice.

- Teacher may decide to use the field work as a focus for the Question Formulation Technique for students to develop group driving questions for future research on local issues. Teacher should be sure to review source credibility, bias, and proper citations.

- Teacher may decide to bring in experts to discuss local issues as a form of field work.

- Teacher will provide a workshop on how to create an infographic as a way to distill group research into the most engaging and simplest format.

2. Voice Poetry

3. Infographic

(Continued)

(Continued)

Benchmark #4: Human Stories/Experiences Related to Community Issues

- Prior to the beginning of this benchmark phase, the teacher will want to identify a location for curating completed student photo essays.
- Come back to NTKs as driver for lessons during this benchmark phase.
- Teacher will introduce students to the concept of photo essays and analyze models using an Artful Thinking Routine.
- Teacher will provide a tech tutorial on how to edit photographs taken during previous field work.
- Teacher will provide a workshop on how to create a photo essay.
- Teacher may decide to have students complete a writing assignment to accompany photographs that includes narratives, subtitles, or informational writing.
- Teacher will ask students to come back to the project DQ as the prompt for developing a photo essay.

4. Photo Essay

Benchmark #5: Civic Engagement

- Come back to NTKs as driver for lessons during this benchmark phase.
- Teacher may choose to cover citizenship and democracy in Greece through engaging history lessons.
- Teacher will discuss the power of our voice and our role as citizens in a democracy. Teacher will help students identify an appropriate government representative or organization recipient for a letter they will be writing to persuade them to take action on a local community issue they have studied.
- Teacher will facilitate a writing workshop on how to write formal letters with a strong claim and reasoning.
- Teacher will take students through the entire writing process.

5. Letter to a Representative

Source: ©2018 Jennifer Piearatt. Project created from First Grade Teacher Team Lake Elementary.

Chapter 7
Assessment in PBL

Best Practices in Assessment Apply to PBL

If you are feeling overwhelmed or unsure about whether PBL can fit into your traditional setting, this deep dive into assessment will hopefully feel familiar to you because a lot of what you are likely already doing, as it relates to assessment, will apply to your project plans. That's right—we don't have to throw the baby out with the bath water here!

> Formative assessment is frequently referred to as "assessment *for* learning"—it needs to occur at frequent intervals throughout a project. Students also need adequate time to revise their work based on feedback, producing multiple drafts of final products as they work toward excellence.
>
> Summative assessment is known as "assessment *of* learning"—it happens at the end of the project (Boss & Larmer, 2018).

The Council of Chief State School Officers (CCSSO) through the Formative Assessment for Students and Teachers State Collaborative on Assessment and Student Standards (FAST SCASS) created a nice, succinct list of the 10 dimensions of best practices in formative assessment, listed here:

- Create Learning Goals
- Define Criteria for Success
- Incorporate Tasks and Activities That Elicit Evidence
- Use Questioning Strategies That Elicit Evidence
- Provide Descriptive Feedback
- Incorporate Peer Feedback
- Incorporate Self-Assessment
- Foster a Collaborative Culture of Learning
- Use Evidence to Inform Instruction

PBL, as a framework, allows all of these dimensions to be fostered throughout the phases of an individual project. Because there are several phases within a project, it makes sense to use a variety of assessment tools to allow for reflection and provide feedback. Brookhart (2016) describes three forms of assessment tools that apply to PBL; Table 7.1 explains when it makes sense to use each of those tools within your project.

● **TABLE 7.1** **Types of Assessment Tools and Possible Uses in Projects**

Definition	Sample Use in a Project
Checklist—A set of criteria that is judged present/absent or yes/no.	Student self-reflection as a quick "reality check" before moving forward to the next step of the project or daily project work.
Rating Scale—A set of criteria that is assessed by a scale (e.g., *excellent, good, poor;* or *always, often, sometimes, never*).	Peer feedback on a draft of project work. Expert panel feedback on a final draft or project "pitch."
Robust Rubric—The use of both criteria and performance-level descriptions.	Shared with students during the project launch to communicate expectations; used for self-reflection and diagnostic feedback during the project; used for evaluation at the end of the project.

How to Build Your Project Rubric

In the spirit of our "big-picture" approach to project planning, we are going to build a robust rubric that considers what you will use to ultimately assess student learning in the project.

Thinking toward the end you have in mind, consider what skills and content students need to master by the time they complete this project. What skills and content should be on display in the final product? These will become the rows of the rubric that you will to create.

Commit to the Content You Will Assess

You have already identified the "big-picture" content you want to cover in this project in the earlier stages of our project planning, so this step is about drilling down beyond the big ideas. You will need to ask yourself

- How many standards do I want to teach, scaffold, assess, and provide feedback for through this project?
- What is *essential* for students to know, and what is simply *nice* for them to know?
- Is this project a vehicle for teaching content, or is it simply a review or extra practice?

Once you decide just how much content you want to cover in this project (typically three content strands), then you will want to build the content rows of your rubric. To do this, copy and paste the language from your standards into the first few rows of your rubric template. The column on the far left (*21st-Century Skill*) will be your big idea, and the "substandards" (written as student deliverables) will be the descriptors under the *Proficient* column.

Use the template provided to help you build your rubric. List relevant twenty-first century skills in the far left and then copy/paste the corresponding text as needed.

Project Rubric Template

21st-Century Skill	Emerging–Developing (1–2)	Proficient (3)	Advanced (4)

Source: ©2018 Jennifer Piearatt

Download this template at resources.corwin.com/keepitrealPBLsecondary

I encourage teachers to create a three-column rubric, unless your district has preexisting rubrics for you to assess your standards. The reason I suggest three columns is because writing assessment descriptors is incredibly difficult to do well, and teasing out the difference between "developing" and "emerging" can easily become an exercise of semantics rather than significant observable student outcomes.

Check out the resources provided on the companion website (resources.corwin.com/keepitrealPBLsecondary) for more help with assessing NGSS.

Now you will need to write the descriptors for the *Developing* and *Advanced* columns. Push yourself to really think about what you would observably *see* a student do (evidence) that is developing or advanced, as it relates to the specific standard. You may even look at the related standards in the grades prior and beyond. You can even use a depth of knowledge or Bloom's taxonomy chart to help you with language (verbs) to write your descriptors. This is a difficult exercise, and I always encourage teachers across grade levels to collaborate on this step of project planning, as it can be a wonderful calibration exercise for vertical alignment across your grade levels.

Assessing the Next Generation Science Standards (NGSS; n.d., 2013, 2015) is a little more involved for this process. Michigan State University (MSU) has a great resource that explains assessment practices and rubric development related to NGSS in an easy-to-understand format. MSU Spark Notes: Start with your Performance Expectations, then unpack Disciplinary Core Ideas, Science and Engineering Practices, and Cross-Cutting Concepts within those to help inform instruction and write out evidence statements of "Learning Performances" as your descriptors in your rubric.

If you are planning an interdisciplinary project with colleagues, here are a few options for building and using your project rubric:

1. You can share a project rubric, meaning each content area instructors place their content in separate rows in the *same* rubric/document. Students can turn in one final product, which is passed among teachers to be assessed for their content area on *one* rubric that "follows" that student.

2. Teachers can also collaboratively grade, meaning they can come together to grade each student product using their own "content area lens" to grade student work while discussing what they see, as evidence of student learning. While this is time-consuming and requires a common planning time, it can be a wonderful way to calibrate on expectations for student work and also identify patterns in student work, which allows increased personalization and support for students.

3. Teachers can create their own individual project rubric, which only includes rows for their own content area. Students can turn in the final product twice (one copy for each teacher), and each teacher grades independently.

Identify the Skills You Will Assess

Similar to how we built the content rows of your rubric, you will now need to think about what twenty-first century skills you hope to foster in your students as a result of this project. Will students be presenting their work at some point, providing an opportunity to scaffold and assess oral communication (CCSS speaking and listening standards)? Will students be asked to work in a group during a phase of the project, thus providing some teachable moments through scaffolding and feedback related to collaboration? While every twenty-first century skill feels important, just pick one or two to focus on for this project. Each of these skills will become one to two additional rows in your project rubric.

Typically, in interdisciplinary projects both teachers agree on the same one or two twenty-first century skills. This serves as a wonderful opportunity for students to be assessed and receive feedback at multiple points by both teachers on these skills within a project.

60

Use the template provided to help you build your rubric. List relevant twenty-first century skills in the far left and then copy/paste the corresponding text as needed.

Project Rubric Template

21st-Century Skill	Emerging–Developing (1–2)	Proficient (3)	Advanced (4)

Source: ©2018 Jennifer Piearatt

 Download this template at resources.corwin.com/keepitrealPBLsecondary

If you are using the recommended expert rubrics for twenty-first century skills, simply copy and paste their language directly into your table (rubric). In Figure 7.1, which contains a complete project rubric for sixth grade, I use the Open Ed Resources provided by New Tech Network for the twenty-first century skills, which can be accessed on the companion website (resources.corwin.com/keepitrealPBLsecondary). You can see more samples of complete-project rubrics (for Grade 9 or 12) that use these similar resources in Appendix A.

Tip: Take it from the experts! Some of my favorite rubrics that align nicely to project-based learning come from **New Tech Network, Envision Schools, PBLWorks, and P21.** Or your district may already have rubrics for twenty-first century skills or your specific content areas. Each of these resources is created by experts in the field of assessment and are proven as valid assessment tools that also embed **Common Core State Standards. You will notice that they do a really nice job of taking something abstract or subjective—such as collaboration or critical thinking—and using concrete language to help both student and teacher align their expectations for a project.**

- What are you biggest pain points when creating a rubric?

- What problems have rubrics helped you avoid in the past?

- Have you ever tried asking students to collaborate to write a rubric of their own? If so, how successful was that?

● **FIGURE 7.1** Sample Project Rubric, Sixth-Grade Humanities Class

21st-Century Skill	Emerging (1)	Developing (2)	Proficient (3)	Advanced (4)
Oral Communication: Use of digital media/visual displays *What is the evidence that the student can use digital media/ visual displays to engage and support audience understanding?*	Digital media or visual displays are confusing, extraneous, or distracting.	Digital media or visual displays are primarily informative and relevant, but some elements are confusing, extraneous, or distracting.	Digital media or visual displays are informative and relevant.	Digital media or visual displays are appealing, informative, and support audience engagement and understanding.
Collaboration: Commitment to shared success	Cannot describe what constitutes success for the team's task. Impedes team progress by failing to complete individual tasks on time. Provides unhelpful negative feedback.	Generally describes what constitutes success in the context of the team's task. Mostly completes individual tasks on time but needs reminding.	Clearly and specifically describes what constitutes success in the context of the team's task. Completes individual tasks on time and with sufficient quality. Provides positive and constructive feedback to team members. Devotes time and effort to ensure team benchmarks and due dates are met.	In addition, . . . Supports others to complete necessary work and ensure the team's success. Actively encourages and motivates others to attain high levels of achievement.
Agency: Impact self and community	Identifies the current status of the classroom and home community but not the ups and downs over time.	Has limited understanding of individual role in the ups and downs of the classroom and home community.	Identifies individual role in the ups and downs of the classroom and home community.	Analyzes individual role in the ups and downs of the classroom and home community.
Written Communication: Development *What is the evidence that the student can develop ideas?*	Does not explain background or context of topic/ issue. Controlling idea* is unclear or not evident throughout the writing. Ideas and evidence are underdeveloped.	Provides a simplistic or partial explanation of background and context of topic/ issue. Controlling idea* is present but unevenly addressed throughout the writing. Ideas and evidence are somewhat developed.	Provides a partial explanation of background and context of topic/ issue. Controlling idea is evident but may not be present throughout the text. Ideas and evidence are mostly developed.	Addresses appropriate background and context of topic/ issue. Controlling idea* is presented clearly throughout the writing. Ideas and evidence are developed.

21st-Century Skill	Emerging (1)	Developing (2)	Proficient (3)	Advanced (4)
Written Communication: Organization *What is the evidence that the student can organize and structure ideas for effective communication?*	Ideas and evidence are disorganized, making relationships unclear. No transitions are used, or are used ineffectively. Conclusion, when appropriate, is absent or restates the introduction or prompt.	Ideas and evidence are loosely sequenced or organized; there is some sense of relationships. Transitions connect ideas with some lapses; may be repetitive or formulaic. Conclusion, when appropriate, follows from the controlling idea.	Ideas and evidence are organized to show relationships, though organization may be formulaic. Transitions connect ideas. Conclusion, when appropriate, follows from and supports the controlling idea.	Ideas and evidence are sequenced to show relationships. Transitions are varied and connect ideas, showing clear relationships. Conclusion, when appropriate, is logical and raises important implications.
Written Communication: Language and conventions *What is the evidence that the student can use language skillfully to communicate ideas?*	Language, style, and tone are inappropriate to the purpose, task, and audience. Uses norms and conventions of writing that are inappropriate to the discipline/genre. ** Has an accumulation of errors in grammar, usage, and mechanics that distract or interfere with meaning. Textual citation, when appropriate, is missing or incorrect.	Language, style, and tone are somewhat appropriate to the purpose, task, and audience. Uses norms and conventions of writing that are mostly inappropriate to the discipline/genre. ** Has some minor errors in grammar, usage, and mechanics that partially distract or interfere with meaning. Cites textual evidence, partially or using an incorrect format, when appropriate.	Language and tone are mostly appropriate to the purpose, task, and audience. Attempts to follow the norms and conventions of writing in the discipline/genre. ** Is generally free of distracting errors in grammar, usage, and mechanics. Cites textual evidence with some errors, when appropriate.	Language, style, and tone are appropriate to the purpose, task, and audience. Follows the norms and conventions of writing in the discipline/genre ** with some errors. Is free of distracting errors in grammar, usage, and mechanics. Cites textual evidence with some minor errors, when appropriate.
Social Studies: Early Humans, Human Behavior	Student is developing in ability to describe and connect early physical and cultural developments across time periods. Student may have limited recall of content vocabulary, events, and locations. Student may not be able to discuss impacts of key events.	6.1 Student can describe what is known through archaeological studies of the early physical and cultural development of humankind from the Paleolithic era to the agricultural revolution. Describe the hunter-gatherer societies, including the development of tools and the use of fire.	In addition, . . . Makes connections to modern-day local community issues.	In addition, . . . Makes connections to modern global issues. Uses supposition to predict the potential future impact.

(Continued)

21st-Century Skill	Emerging (1)	Developing (2)	Proficient (3)	Advanced (4)
		Identify the locations of human communities that populated the major regions of the world and describe how humans adapted to a variety of environments. Discuss the climatic changes and human modifications of the physical environment that gave rise to the domestication of plants and animals and new sources of clothing and shelter.		
Social Studies: Citizenship	Student is developing in ability to analyze the geographic, political, economic, religious, and social structures of early civilizations of Ancient Greece. Student may struggle to make connections or comparisons.	6.4 Student can analyze the geographic, political, economic, religious, and social structures of the early civilizations of Ancient Greece. Trace the transition from tyranny and oligarchy to early democratic forms of government and back to dictatorship in ancient Greece, including the significance of the invention of the idea of citizenship (e.g., from Pericles' Funeral Oration). State the key differences between Athenian, or direct, democracy and representative democracy.	In addition, . . . Makes the connection to modern-day citizenship and participation.	In addition, . . . Articulates one's individual role in a democracy.
ELA Research: Research to build and present knowledge	Student is not yet able to conduct research projects independently.	CCSS.ELA-LITERACY.W.6.7 Conduct short research projects to answer a question, drawing on several sources and refocusing the inquiry when appropriate.	In addition, . . . Makes further inquiry through additional research questions.	In addition, . . . Engages in lengthier research projects driven by complexity of inquiry and interest.

21st-Century Skill	Emerging (1)	Developing (2)	Proficient (3)	Advanced (4)
	Student is able to gather information from a single source, but may struggle to assess its credibility and/or effectively paraphrase the content. Student is developing in ability to draw upon data to support his or her reflection, analysis, or research.	CCSS.ELA-LITERACY.W.6.8 Gather relevant information from multiple print and digital sources; assess the credibility of each source; and quote or paraphrase the data and conclusions of others while avoiding plagiarism and providing basic bibliographic information for sources. CCSS.ELA-LITERACY.W.6.9 Draw evidence from literary or informational texts to support analysis, reflection, and research.	Gathers information from guest speakers and shows proper citations when paraphrasing. Draws evidence from a wide variety of sources to support analysis, reflection, and research.	Gathers information from nontraditional sources through independent field work interactions. Properly paraphrases, documents, and cites such interactions. Draws evidence from a variety of sources, including field work, to support analysis, reflection, and research.

Source: Original rubrics created by New Tech Network with support from Stanford Center for Assessment, Learning, and Equity (SCALE) and based on similar rubrics from Envision Schools. @Copyright New Tech Network 2016. Modifications to rubric made by CraftED Curriculum, LLC, in support of project design for Innovate Public Schools.

 Download the blank template at resources.corwin.com/keepitrealPBLsecondary

#realtalk: Whoa, that's a big rubric! This rubric may be a little overwhelming when you start to put it all together, but know that what you're creating will not be used in its entirety. You're actually going to use just a few rows at a time to provide formative feedback to students at each benchmarking phase you identified in the last chapter.

Planning for Formative Assessment

This step is one that teachers often want to skip over because they assume that they have covered all their bases by this point, but it is a huge safety net that I would strongly encourage you to take the time to complete. Go back to your benchmark deliverables that we planned from the last chapter. You will now need to "map" them onto the rows of your rubric. This exercise ensures that each row of your rubric is being used at multiple points throughout the project. This is important so that students have multiple opportunities to receive feedback *for* learning, to allow them to grow. Figures 7.2A and 7.2B show ways you can do this exercise, and Figure 7.3 shows a completed sample.

● FIGURE 7.2A You can hand-draw a quick rubric frame to be sure that each benchmark (labeled on the far left) maps onto the rows of your rubric. You can even color-coordinate your benchmarks and arrows to help you see which benchmark go with which rows.

	Approaching standards	Meeting standards	Above standards
ELA-CCSS			
NGSS 5 Ess3-1 5 LS 1			
Collaboration			
Agency- growth mindset			
Oral and written communication			

B1 Labeled Diagram
B2 Labeled Diagram
B3 Storyboard, script
B4 Film

● FIGURE 7.2B You may prefer to use sticky notes for your benchmark mapping exercise. Simply make a rubric frame with the rows and columns of your rubric, and then write each benchmark number on a sticky note and place them on the rows that align.

	Emerging	Proficient	Advanced
ELA-CCSS:	Benchmark 3 Benchmark 1		
ELA-CCSS	Benchmark 2 Benchmark 1		
Collaboration	Benchmark 3 Benchmark 5		

	Emerging	Proficient	Advanced
Social Studies	Benchmark 2 Benchmark 4		
ELA-CCSS	Benchmark 3 Benchmark 5		
Oral Communication	Benchmark 4 Benchmark 5		

● FIGURE 7.3 Sample Benchmarking Assessment Mapping Exercise for Sixth-Grade Humanities Project

Benchmark: Deliverable	Rubric Rows for Formative Assessment
#1 Early Humans: Narrative	Written Communication: Language and conventions SS: Early Humans, Human Behavior
#2 Compare/Contrast: 2 Voice Poetry	Written Communication: Organization and collaboration Oral Communication: Use of digital media/visual displays SS: Early Humans, Human Behavior
#3 Community Issues: Infographic	Collaboration ELA research
#4 Human Stories: Photo essay	Collaboration Agency: Impact self and community Agency: Use effort to practice and grow Oral Communication: Use of digital media/visual displays Written communication: Language and conventions
#5 Civic Engagement: Letter to representative	Written Communication: Development Written Communication: Language and conventions Agency: Impact self and community Agency: Use effort to practice and grow

If as you are doing this mapping exercise you notice that your benchmarks either didn't map onto a row of your rubric, some rows mapped onto every benchmark, or a rubric row didn't map onto a benchmark, this is a good reality check for you. Go back to the early stages of project planning. Do your EU (enduring understanding) and DQ (driving question) truly elicit the performance expectations you created in your rubric? Look at your benchmark plans; do they truly act as a stepping stone to help students master the content and skills you are hoping to assess by the end of the project? If not, then fine-tune your project plans before moving forward.

Would you believe there is a "rubric for a rubric"? PBLWorks has created a rubric for your rubric that I like to use with colleagues to help each other analyze their assessment tool to provide feedback to one another. It is available on the companion website (resources.corwin .com/keepitrealPBLsecondary).

FAQ: What's Worth Assessing?

1. Should I grade for grammar?

If grammar is something you are working on in ELA and you would like to use a project benchmark as "double duty" to grade grammar, then go for it. The grammar grade will be separate from the project grade and will not appear on the rubric, but you can use the project work as context/practice for grammar and review in a separate grammar lesson. If you are a science teacher, you can decide if you want to do a grammar lesson (maybe with the help or direction from an ELA colleague) and grade for grammar, or you can just focus on your content and turn a blind eye to grammar.

2. Does handwriting count?

If you are teaching and assessing handwriting, then—similar to the grammar question previously— you can use project benchmarks or products as context for "double duty." Again, this grade will not appear on the rubric and will be separate from the project .

3. I teach science, not ELA, but the writing my students turn in for project work is terrible. What is my role in grading their writing?

I actually get this question a lot, and I typically reply with a few options for teachers: (1) Perhaps you can buddy up with the ELA teacher and ask her or him to do a few lessons in English class on the technical writing you are asking students to do; (2) perhaps that same buddy ELA teacher will even assess student writing for your assignment and give them a grade in his or her class; (3) you can take the time to teach them technical, scientific writing. And if you don't know how to do that, ask an ELA colleague to give you some pointers or resources to help you better scaffold this skill.

4. What if a student didn't contribute to the group final product—how do I grade them?

Group grades are a "no-no" in PBL. Remember that benchmarks should be individual assessments of student knowledge and skills. If they aren't pulling their weight in a group, then you will give them feedback using the collaboration row of your rubric.

5. What if students don't show mastery on a benchmark? Do I let them go ahead?

No! If students move ahead, they will be moving on a faulty foundation for the project. There will likely be a few students who may not show proficiency when you do a formative assessment. You can pull these individuals to do small-group instruction to support them. Workshop model during project work time is a great way to facilitate this process (see Chapter 8).

Student Engagement in PBL Assessment

Engaging students in the assessment process is critical in PBL. By involving students through self-reflection, peer feedback, diagnostic teacher feedback, and conferencing, the following are assured:

1. *Increased odds for "closing the gap."* Boaler and Confer (n.d.) explain that "well-crafted tasks and questions, accompanied by clear feedback, offer students a growth mindset pathway that helps them know that they can learn at high levels and, critically, how they can get there" (p. 2). Again, when we communicate our expectations (through the use of a well-designed rubric) and provide students feedback on their growth, it is very clear what steps they need to take to develop.

2. *Student ownership.* Students can be leaders of their learning when they are provided ongoing feedback and opportunities to get better. They are able to set goals, ask specific questions, and take actionable steps independently, thus increasing student agency.

3. *Assessment* for *learning.* Through formative assessment practices, students have the opportunity to keep trying and grow from ongoing feedback, rather than waiting until the end of a project to receive feedback; by then, it's too late for students to make the small shifts needed to improve.

One of Hattie's most highly ranked "influences on achievement" was providing students feedback on their learning, as Larmer (2016b) explains:

> Students must understand feedback as something intended to help them improve, not a judgement of their competency or worth. . . [furthermore], effective feedback is useful, timely, understandable, and clear in pointing out the things students can do better. It is also presented in a way that students do not find disparaging. (para. 17)

Brookhart (2016) offers a list of ways students can engage in the rubric assessment process (see Table 7.2).

● **TABLE 7.2** Strategies for Using Rubrics With Students

Strategies to Use Before Work Begins/ When Assignment Is Introduced	Strategies to Use After Work Begins/As Learning Is Happening
Ask students to pose clarifying questions.	Have students match their own or peers' work to the rubrics and explain their reasoning.
Ask students to restate the rubric in their own words.	Have students use a highlighter to match performance descriptions to elements in their work.
	Use rubrics to help students keep track of their own work.

Source: Adapted from Brookhart (2016).

Depending on what age your students are, they may or may not be able to engage with the language as it stands in your rubric since it is probably pretty teacher-specific. Especially for middle school teachers, I recommend creating a student-facing rubric that takes the language of your standards and skills (row by row from your rubric) and puts them into simple "I-can" statements. Two examples are provided in Figures 7.4 and 7.5.

● **FIGURE 7.4** Sample Student-Facing Rubric, Sixth-Grade Science

I can define the criteria and constraints of a design problem by considering scientific principles and potential impact.

NGSS Engineering

I can develop a model to test and go through iterations for improvement.

Body Systems

I can gather and briefly summarize information that sensory receptors are responsible for.

● **FIGURE 7.5** Sample Student-Facing Rubric, Seventh-Grade Science

Student: _____

Period: _____

Success Criteria:

I can distinguish between manipulated and responding variables in an experiment.

1: Beginning	2: Developing	3: Emerging	4: Expert
I cannot do this.	I can do this with assistance.	I can do this on my own.	I can teach this to someone.

Success Criteria:

I can design an experiment with controls, variables, and constants.

1: Beginning	2: Developing	3: Emerging	4: Expert
I cannot do this.	I can do this with assistance.	I can do this on my own.	I can teach this to someone.

For upper grades, an in-depth self-assessment activity could look like the sample from a 10th-grade humanities project called "Back Off, You Big Bully" in Figure 7.6.

● **FIGURE 7.6** **"Back Off, You Big Bully"—Mid-Project Reflection**

Instructions: Make a copy for yourself and do not share this with your team. Answer the questions as completely as possible and submit by linking this Google Doc through the submission box in Echo.

1. In your own words, what will you be teaching the class during your WWII minipresentation?

2. List some difficult concepts from your topic that you think will be hard for the class to understand.

3. List all of the things you did to learn about your topic.

4. What is something you wish you would have done differently this week?

5. Describe and reflect on how well you are meeting the schoolwide learning outcomes of *Knowledge and Thinking* (the ability to learn by reading and writing) and *Agency* (ability to meet deadlines and having a growth mindset)?

6. Please evaluate each of your team members using the New Tech Network Collaboration Rubric found at newtechnetwork.org. (collab. 10 pts). Highlight or **bold** the score you think they deserve for each set of criteria. Please score yourself, too.

Yet another approach to self-reflection and assessment from a 12th-grade AP government class uses the New Tech Network Team Collaboration Checklist and New Tech Network Collaboration Rubric High School both available at newtechnetwork.org. These rubrics use a checklist format, based on language of a teacher rubric to evaluate a peer on their collaboration. A more simplified daily self-reflection/assessment is found in the form of an exit ticket in Figure 7.7.

● **FIGURE 7.7** **Exit Ticket for Self-Reflection**

● *What do you notice that is similar about the content of the presentations today?*

● *In your opinion, is there a "one-size-fits-all" solution to the problem of fixing governments?*

● *What are your big takeaways about working in a group and what you do/don't do well?*

For science teachers, check out the K–12 Alliance NGSS resources provided on the companion website (resources.corwin.com/ keepitrealPBLsecondary). They provide all cross-cutting concepts as "I-can statement" rubrics ready for you to use!

Use the template provided by referencing your teacher-facing rubric and rewriting each row as a learning target in student-friendly language.

Student Project Rubric Template

	Not Yet	Most of the Time	Always
I can …	😐	🙂	😀
I can …	😐	🙂	😀
I can …	😐	🙂	😀
I can …	😐	🙂	😀
I can …	😐	🙂	😀
I can …	😐	🙂	😀

Source: Adapted from PBLWorks Presentation Rubric ©2011.

 Download a blank version of this template at resources.corwin.com/keepitrealPBLsecondary

The blank student rubric above lets you do any of the following reflection and self-assessment activities:

- Complete written self-reflections as journal entries or exit tickets.
- Provide specific peer feedback using rubric language.
- Sort sample student work according to the columns of your rubric.
- Document growth using benchmark formative assessments and reflection for parent–teacher or student-led conferences.

A few other best-assessment practices I have seen in PBL include the following:

- Give teacher feedback using an individual row of the rubric—either using a highlighter, the highlight feature in a Google Doc, or writing comments (or using the comment feature in Google Docs)—to show where students currently stand.

- Use language of the rubric to create a checklist for students to quickly self-assess as an exit ticket or project work time management strategy. This same checklist, or scale, can be used for peer or expert feedback

- Ask students to create SMART (specific, measurable, attainable, relevant, and timely) goals based off language in the teacher or student rubric.

- Use the language of the rubric to do a class "looks like, sounds like, feels like" chart to leave up in the classroom to help guide students.

#realtalk: Group grades are not a best practice in PBL. Oftentimes, teachers will think that because a project is collaborative, students should receive group grades. You always want to individually assess student knowledge and skills. As for the group work part of a project, use a collaboration rubric to evaluate each student on the subskills of collaboration (how well do they listen to peers' ideas, etc.).

#realtalk: Time out! If you have six to seven periods a day with class sizes anywhere from 30 to 45 students, you are probably wondering, *How am I supposed to grade every student multiple times with this big rubric AND also ask them to self-reflect?!* In the interview with Aaron Sottile, and also in Appendix A, you will find some tips from the trenches on how to get a handle on assessment in PBL when you are juggling large student caseloads at any secondary grade level.

Teacher Interview

With Aaron Sottile, Grades 7–8 Science Teacher at Calavera Hills Middle School (a large, comprehensive middle school in Carlsbad, California)

Q1: What has been your biggest "Aha!" related to assessment in PBL?

It seemed really daunting at first, but I'm starting to feel like it's more doable now that I have **systems** in place. I have found that using **technology** is really helpful for these systems because I have so many students. I like using Google Forms because it allows me to embed opportunities for student self-reflection into my short class period through a simple digital "do now" or an exit ticket. For example, the day after we launched our rockets I asked them to evaluate their collaboration and provide evidence for why/how they scored themselves using Google Sheets. It's not a perfect system yet, and I have gone through three iterations before landing on the one that works for me:

1. On one iteration, it was **"grade yourself."** Surprisingly, they were really honest about evaluating themselves, which is great because I can't be there for every step of their project. This was also great because it provided documentation in writing, which is also terrific for IEP meetings (their struggles and goals, in their own words).

2. The next iteration was **"me grade them" and compare** with their own self/student grade. This was great because we could compare how I saw them and how they saw themselves prior to me entering a grade into my gradebook.

3. On the third iteration, I **took off the numbers on the rubric** and just left the descriptive language. I like this the best because they aren't being swayed by the grade/number. I think they are more honest when they just say "I'm proficient" compared to, say, a "5–6 points." I have also learned to **give them a copy of their responses** (via "Response Receipts" in Google), which can be really helpful later in the semester or with digital portfolios.

Q2: What do you find to be the biggest challenge with formatively assessing all of your students during a project? And how to you address that challenge?

It's difficult to provide frequent feedback when there are so many layers to the project—it can easily feel like a beast! I am constantly wrestling between what's most important to assess: content, soft skills, and so on.

To cut down those layers, I—as a science teacher—**first look at the disciplinary core ideas** and try to land on which of the science and engineering practices are most applicable. I have to decide which type of learning matches best with which of the standards, and of those, which matches best with PBL—and all content doesn't always go with PBL. There are many ways to address the standards; you have to decide what's most authentic.

(Continued)

(Continued)

And then, from a 30,000-foot view, I wonder, *Am I covering enough?* I interact a lot with **other people in my department** (10 times a year we meet as a department), and we try to decide how to share the load; we look at our students on a continuum across their three years with us. No one person can do it alone, so we have to work together to focus on deep dives (of specific DCIs and SEPs to assess), one year at a time. It's not perfect, but it has made assessment in general feel more doable because it celebrates depth not breadth, and that helps a lot with PBL.

Sample Science Department Vertical Planning

🔖 CHMS Cross-Cutting Concepts Progression		
All Grade Levels Each Year		
Cause and Effect		
Scale, Quantity, and Proportion		
6th Grade	7th Grade	8th Grade
Structure and Function	Stability and Change	Patterns
Systems and System Models	Energy and Matter	Science, Engineering, and Technology Influence on the Natural World

Q3: What is the most efficient way you have figured out how to give feedback to students on benchmarks?

When they present, I give active feedback on the rubric right then and there. I use Google Classroom, and I type feedback on digital rubrics or I print out rubrics. By the time students are done presenting, I am done with feedback, and that is a great feeling! During the presentations, I use **shortcuts in ProKeys**, and that is super helpful, too. After running a project, you have a pretty good idea of what feedback you are going to give students (where they struggled), and it ends up being the same over and over again! For example, I have the shortcut "Provide more detail to clearly explain your message; see rubric for ideas," and then I give them a link to the rubric as a scaffold to help them. I simply use my shortcut—I probably used that one 20 times in the last round of presentations.

I also **create systems**; for example, the day after every test or project end we do a digital project reflection. When students are familiar with these systems, they know what to expect. I do these student reflections in Google Classroom, which is nice because it allows it to be personal and it stays about their own work and effort. I let students give themselves a grade, then I give a grade, and then I look to see if they match up before I put it in the gradebook.

Q4: How do students engage with project rubrics in your class?

I don't do student-facing rubrics, just because of personal preference. First, I do a **readability test** on my rubric online, and it tells me the grade level of the writing—I often find that they are too high for my eighth-grade students to understand. I use that data to help me drive **calibration conversations**. I take the time to preview the rubric with students at the beginning of the project; we have to calibrate on rubric language—"What does that mean? What does that look like?"

We have **debrief conversations** often, coming back to the language in the rubric.

They **write/type about their progress** during project reflections, and we do those periodically, with a big one at the end of the project.

Q5: What have you found is the value in asking students to self-reflect, as it relates to assessment in project work?

When you read what students write, it's really **authentic.** They are talking about their own learning in the first person, and that depth doesn't normally happen unless you give them the opportunity to do so. My quiet students and EL kids often surprise me—it's really neat to see. You wonder if stuff is getting through, but then you read their reflections and you are like, "Wow, they got it." Their responses also serve as a **priority list** for me—to see who I need to focus on that needs help/guidance.

Q6: What does interdisciplinary assessment look like for you?

Well, it starts with **"hallway talk."** We don't have a structured time to make rubrics or assess students together. At our school, we teach with our doors open so we all know what's going on in each other's rooms—this helps us make natural connections across content areas.

I have done a few interdisciplinary projects. In a recent science project, their background research was done in ELA (in that case, the ELA teacher graded them on their research skills and writing, and I graded them on the science content). **We used two different rubrics and gave them their respective grades for each class**. The ELA teacher also helped by teaching me better research structure, which allowed us to have synergy, so that students got the same message and support in both classes.

With our current rocket project, I'm collaborating with the math teacher. We collect the data in science, and they analyze it in math. Those groups are actually different in each class because of the way students' schedules work, but it's actually cool because they get to see various groups and more practice by seeing their own data and their other group

(Continued)

(Continued)

members' data. If students are struggling with one concept in science, it likely carries over to math, and I can communicate that to the teacher to be sure that student gets extra help. **We don't use a rubric for this; we just put the grades in our respective gradebooks**. It's been great because now I don't have to cover the math in my class, and my students appreciate it because it saves them time, too.

Our school is launching a **schoolwide collaboration rubric** that we all will be using in differentiated ways by grade level. That will cut across disciplines and is also an example of interdisciplinary assessment.

Q7: What's the one thing you think teachers new to PBL should know about assessment?

Figure out a system that works for you and don't be afraid to make changes. Do it right then—don't wait until next year. This is true for your teaching practice, too—if something isn't working, make the change right away! When you frequently assess benchmarks, it allows you to see if something isn't working because you can see where students are struggling. Then you can reteach and develop new systems to put in place to help next time around.

Chapter 8
Planning Daily Learning in PBL

Create Your Big-Picture Project Calendar

When first building your calendar, remain in "big-picture mode"—don't get caught up in day-to-day lessons yet. Approaching your project calendar in this way will help you realistically pace yourself (without getting overwhelmed) by first seeing how many weeks each of your benchmarks will take, thus guiding your overall project timeline. To pace your benchmarks, start by asking yourself a series of questions:

- How long does teaching this content typically take?
- Will this be the vehicle for teaching this content or a review?
- Do we have any holidays or major school events during this time period?
- Will I be using instructional minutes for more than one content area within a given day?

How you answer these questions will give you a general guideline for how long each benchmark will take. As you begin to pace out your benchmarks, you can simply make a note on the far left column of your blank calendar, noting the week(s) designated for each benchmark.

Figures 8.1 and 8.2 are sample sixth-grade (humanities) and 12th-grade (AP government) project calendars. Notice that the calendars are in "big-picture mode," meaning they don't have the specific lesson plans, but rather, they are built similarly to a road map with guidelines and topics for project pacing.

You may consider using a Google Document with the table feature for your calendar. By doing this, you are able to make responsive changes to your students, and those changes are saved in real time; that way, parents, team teachers, or your school administrator can easily see an accurate picture of what's happening daily in your project. It also is an easy way to link daily resources, which makes planning the project the second time around that much easier!

● **FIGURE 8.1 Sixth-Grade Humanities Project Calendar**

The Human Experience: Past to Present

	Monday	Tuesday	Wednesday	Thursday	Friday
Week 1 Benchmark #1	Project launch!	Early humans	Early humans	Early humans	Complete case study profile
Week 2 Benchmark #1	WW: Narrative writing, brainstorm	Complete narrative writing draft #1	Revise narrative writing (self, peer)	Draft #2 of narrative writing	**Benchmark #1 due: Complete narrative writing**
Week 3 Benchmark #2	Intro to local issues	Walking field trip	Identify group topics for research via QFT process	Group research	Group research
Week 4 Benchmark #2	Prep for field work interviews	Turn in interview questions, role-play	Conduct field work interviews	Debrief interviews	**Benchmark #2 due: Venn diagram**
Week 5 Benchmark #3	WW: Intro to 2 voice poetry	Revise writing	Audio record	Edits	**Benchmark #3 due: Final 2 voice poetry due**
Week 6 Benchmark #4	Additional group research	Experts visit, field work	WW: citations	Intro to infographics	Group work on infographics
Week 7 Benchmark #4	Group work on infographics	**Benchmark #4 due: Groups turn in infographics**	Intro to photo editing	Digital edits	WW: Photo essays
Week 8 Benchmark #5	Draft #1 of photo essays	Revisions, feedback (self, peer)	Draft #2 of photo essays	**Benchmark #5 due: Photo essays**	
Week 9 Benchmark #6/final	Lesson: Our voice, identifying recipient	WW: Formal letter (claim, persuasive language, effective comm.)	Draft #1 of letter	Revisions, feedback (self, peer)	**Final due: Draft #2 of letter**
Week 10	Exhibition prep and final project reflections			Exhibition	

*WW: Writers' Workshop

• FIGURE 8.2 12th-Grade Project Calendar for Political Party Simulation

	Day 1	Day 2	Day 3	Day 4	Day 5
Week 1 Launch	Roll out project K/NTK	Intro to the Indiana house: political survey results Notes on political spectrum	History of political parties	Democrat party platform Republican party platform Libertarian party platform Sort	Get in groups Group work day Introduce organizer/rubric
Week 2 Benchmark #1	Major issues for the current election (state and federal)	Elected office at federal, state, local level	Research . . . Where do the candidates stand?	Review	**Benchmark #1 due: Major parties and political ideology test**
Week 3 Benchmark #2	Group work day Develop party platform	Group work day Develop party platform Start promotion	Group work day Identify candidate/Work on promotional material **Benchmark #2: Promotional material due**	History of interest groups and campaigns in the United States	Group work day
Week 4 Benchmark #3	Speechwriting workshop for candidates	Promotion/Group work day	Campaign day/Group work day **Benchmark #3: Speeches due**	Campaign day/Speeches to electorate	Election Day

Daily Learning

Once you have the benchmarks listed, then you can begin to identify daily learning targets, workshops, labs, or other learning activities to help students master content and skills for each benchmark. This is where scaffolding comes into play, so reference your rubric to help you think about your end in mind—what skills and content will you need to break down for students so they are prepared for each benchmark and, ultimately, the final product or experience?

For secondary teachers, daily learning can often become especially challenging due to limited time periods with students, large class caseloads, and additional challenges when co-planning with colleagues on interdisciplinary projects. For this reason, the organization of daily project planning is critical; and in this case, the more information the better! Notice the level of detail in the sample daily lesson calendar in Figure 8.3, which drills one level down (with all teacher daily lesson plans) from the project calendar in Figure 8.2 (*Note:* Color coordination corresponds to different content areas). The blank project calendar in Figure 8.4 is provided for your use.

● **FIGURE 8.3** **Sample Daily Lesson Project Calendar**

10th-Grade Interdisciplinary Project

Monday 4/29	Tuesday 4/30–Wednesday 5/1	Thursday 5/2–Friday 5/3
Bio: **Homework:** ● Weekly Calendar **Objective:** Students will review genetics terminology and concepts in preparation for their new unit. **Essential Question:** How can we use our understanding of probability and genetics to make predictions? **Standards:** HS-LS1-1, HS-LS3-1, HS-LS3-2, HS-LS3-3	Bio: **Homework:** ● Weekly Calendar ● Please revise your CRA! CRA feedback. You must turn in your original rubric and resubmit to turnitin.com in order to be rescored. *- Due at the end of the year* ● Punnett square notes & practice problems *- Due by the end of the block*	Bio: **Homework:** ● Weekly Calendar ● Please revise your CRA! CRA feedback. You must turn in your original rubric and resubmit to turnitin.com in order to be rescored. *- Due at the end of the year* ● Finish "The Real CSI" article organizer (hard copy) *- Due Monday (5/6), beginning of class* ● Prepare for investigation team interviews *- Monday (5/6)*

Monday 4/29	Tuesday 4/30– Wednesday 5/1	Thursday 5/2–Friday 5/3
Agenda: • Do Now: NEATure Poster! • Review genetics key terms (Quizlet) • Quizlet Live!	**Objective:** Students will review genetics terminology and concepts in preparation for their new unit. **Essential Question:** How can we use our understanding of probability and genetics to make predictions? **Standards:** HS-LS1-1, HS-LS3-1, HS-LS3-2, HS-LS3-3 **Agenda:** • Do Now: Journal entry (paper) • Explain the relationship between genes, alleles, genotype, and phenotype. Be detailed and specific. (4–5 complete sentences) • Be prepared to share out parts of your journal entry to your table groups and the class. • Punnett square notes & practice problems • Must be completed and stamped by the end of the block! • Guiding Slidedeck • Online web activity: Pigeonetics • Potential extra credit available!	**Objective:** Students will be briefed on "The Case of Mama's Stolen Mug" and will begin setting up investigation teams. **Essential Question:** How can we as students use inquiry and our knowledge of heredity and genetics to solve a crime? **Standards:** HS-LS3-1, CCSS.ELA-LITERACY.RST.9-10.9 **Agenda:** • Do Now: Announcement of crime • Crime Scene Investigation • Roll for prints, blood sample, hair follicle collection • Take pictures, videos, notes (hard copy) • Lead investigator application • "The Real CSI": Article & organizer (hard copy) • Article (*National Geographic* website) • Article (PDF copy) • Lead investigator reveal & interview preparation

Monday 5/6	Tuesday 5/7– Wednesday 5/8	Thursday 5/9–Friday 5/10
Bio: **Homework:** • Weekly Calendar • Please revise your CRA! CRA feedback. You must turn in your original rubric and resubmit to turnitin.com in order to be rescored. **- Due at the end of the year** • <u>**Due:**</u> The Real CSI article organizer (hardcopy) • Bring board/poster for your team's investigation board **- For Thurs/Fri.** **Objective:** Students will commence with investigation team interviews.	Bio: **Homework:** • Weekly Calendar • Please revise your CRA! CRA feedback. You must turn in your original rubric and resubmit to turnitin.com in order to be rescored. **- Due at the end of the year** • Bring board/poster for your team's investigation board **- For Thurs/Fri.** **Objective:** Students will go over project guidelines and set themselves up for a successful final project.	Bio: **Homework:** • Weekly Calendar • Please revise your CRA! CRA feedback. You must turn in your original rubric and resubmit to turnitin.com in order to be rescored. **- Due at the end of the year** • Benchmark #1: Fingerprinting Subpoena **- Due in class today!** • Begin Benchmark #4 (IAKT): Summary of Evidence (Ultimately, your arrest warrant!) • Complete <u>Part II: Fingerprinting</u> **ONLY**

(Continued)

(Continued)

Monday 5/6	Tuesday 5/7– Wednesday 5/8	Thursday 5/9–Friday 5/10

Essential Question: How can we best prepare for a team interview?
 	
Standard: HS-LS3-1, CCSS.ELA-LITERACY.RST.9-10.9
 	
Agenda:
 	
• Do Now: NEATure
• Stamp article organizer
• Investigation team interviews
• Investigation questions
 	
R&C
 	
Objective:
 	
Students will meet their new teams for the CSI Forensics project and update their professional portfolio websites with WWI reflections.
 	
EQ:
 	
What does it take to make a film?
 	
Today:
 	
• Meet new teams (what's your favorite movie trailer and why?)
• Pass back all rubrics
• Check gradebook! Do you need to show me your IAKT?
• Get digitally organized *Upload any pics/video* to your professional portfolio website.
• WWI Reflection Form that you are doing in World Studies . . . use what you wrote and copy and paste it on your Professional Portfolio website (this is the guiding doc, but you already typed it up in the Google form: IAKT: Selecting Artifacts & Reflecting)
• Press article
• 2019 photo essays!!!
 	
Additional Tasks:
 	
• Deep Dive: Create a This Is Me photo essay to put on your website!
	Essential Question: How can fingerprints be reliable and unreliable sources of evidence?
	
	Standard: HS-LS3-1, CCSS.ELA-LITERACY.RST.9-10.10
	
	Agenda:
	
	• Do Now: Read over the Agency Log
	• Make an individual copy
	• Make your first entry (investigation leads exempt)
	• Investigation team selection
	• Team reveal!
	• Project guidelines
	• Knows, need to knows, next steps (team hard copy)
	• Project Housekeeping:
	  ○ Complete team contracts
	  ○ Set up team drawer
	  ○ Set up team folder
	• Fingerprinting 101! Begin fingerprinting pre-lab (hard copy)
	
	R&C
	
	Objective:
	
	Students will deconstruct film trailers and debrief project guidelines in order to understand how to complete the CSI Forensics project successfully.
	
	EQ:
	
	What does it take to make a film?
	
	Today:
	
	• Jump start: Meet new teams & in your journal respond to the following: Who are you? If your life were to be made into a movie this summer, what would the story line be? What would the genre be? What songs would appear on the soundtrack?
	• Entry event & debrief: Trailer example deconstruction (take notes in your journal)
		• Bio Spring Final is **Wed/Thurs of finals week!** Complete the study guide by hand, and you can use it on the exam!
		
		Objective: Students will start tracking their agency and will practice identifying fingerprint types.
		
		Essential Question: How can fingerprints be reliable and unreliable sources of information?
		
		Standard: HS-LS3-1, 3-3, CCSS.ELA-LITERACY.RST.9-10.4
		
		Agenda:
		
		• Do Now: Agency Log
		• Finish Fingerprinting 101! Video 1 and Video 2
		• Take Cornell notes!
		• Complete Fingerprinting pre-lab (hard copy)
		• Fingerprinting lab! As a team, examine the fingerprint slides for all your suspects and determine if the prints are loops, arches, or whirls. Record all your findings on your team Suspect List.
		• Benchmark #1: Fingerprinting Subpoena
		  ○ This is an individual assignment!
		  ○ Due in class today!
		  ○ Submit here
		• Begin investigation boards
		• Suspect list
		• Suspect photos
		• Begin Benchmark #4 (IAKT): Summary of Evidence (Ultimately, your arrest warrant!)
		• Complete Part II: Fingerprinting **ONLY**
		• Exit ticket: Complete the reflection box of your Agency log

Monday 5/6	Tuesday 5/7–Wednesday 5/8	Thursday 5/9–Friday 5/10
	<ul><li>Project guidelines</li><li>Intro Benchmark One: Team Organization (Team Contracts) - **Due at the end of your next R&C block**</li><li>Watch Trello demo video (put the Trello link on your organization doc)</li><li>Create a Trello account</li><li>Watch Trello demo video **again plugged in if you need to**</li><li>Upload capture crime scene and other footage to your Google Drive</li><li>Exit ticket: Trello board</li></ul>**Additional Tasks:**<ul><li>**DUE FRIDAY!!!** WWI Reflection Form that you did in World Studies . . . use what you wrote and copy and paste it on your Professional Portfolio website (this is the guiding doc but you already typed it up in the Google form: IAKT: Selecting Artifacts & Reflecting).</li><li>Press article</li><li>2019 photo essays!!!</li><li>Deep Dive: create a This Is Me photo essay to put on your website!</li><li>Reminders: Take footage (film & still frames) of labs in biology & link to Organization Doc & link to K/NTKs</li></ul>	**R&C** *Objective:* *Students will learn about some film making basics and work to organize their team by working on Benchmark One.* *EQ:* *What does it take to make a film?* **Today:**<ul><li>Jump start: Watch vertical video syndrome & read "How to Make a Movie" article & watch 2018 Example 1 and Example 2 . . . feel free to pick 1 or 2 more examples of 2017–18 trailers (you can plug in with headphones for this).</li><li>Add to K/NTKs (Project Guidelines)</li><li>Update Trello</li><li>**Work time for Benchmark One: Team Organization DUE**</li><li>Upload capture crime scene and other footage to your Google Drive</li><li>Need WeVideo? See me.</li><li>Work time for Benchmark Two: CSI Screenplay, Storyboard, & Moodboard (do this however you want, on the bottom of your organization doc, on a separate doc or slide show or on paper)</li><li>Filmmaking Resources: This will help! Use the Storyclock for writers.</li><li>Exit ticket: Update Trello board & fill out song survey for the Academy Awards pre-party</li></ul>**Additional Tasks:**<ul><li>**DUE FRIDAY!!!** WWI Reflection Form that you did in World Studies . . . use what you wrote and copy and paste it on your Professional Portfolio website (this is the guiding doc but you already typed it up in the Google form: IAKT: Selecting Artifacts & Reflecting)</li><li>Press article</li><li>2019 photo essays!!!</li></ul>

(Continued)

(Continued)

Monday 5/6	Tuesday 5/7– Wednesday 5/8	Thursday 5/9–Friday 5/10
		<ul><li>Link to photos</li><li>Benchmark Two Due 5/14 or 5/15</li><li>Deep Dive: create a This Is Me photo essay to put on your website!</li><li>Reminders: Take footage (film & still frames) of labs in biology & link to Organization Doc & link to K/NTKs</li><li>Example Storyboard</li><li>Example Moodboard</li><li>Example Screenplay</li><li>Filmmaking Resources</li><li>Understanding camera basics</li><li>2016–17 trailers</li><li>2017–18 trailers</li></ul>

Monday 5/13 (No class)	Tuesday 5/14– Wednesday 5/15 (89-minute blocks)	Thursday 5/16 (44-minute periods)
Bio: **Homework:**<ul><li>Weekly Calendar</li><li>All late work and revisions - **Due Wednesday June 6th at 12pm**</li><li>Begin Benchmark #4 (IAKT): Summary of Evidence (Ultimately, your arrest warrant!)</li><li>Complete <u>Part II: Fingerprinting</u> **ONLY**</li><li>Bio Spring Final is **Wed/Thurs of finals week!** Complete the study guide by hand, and you can use it on the exam!</li></ul> **Agenda:** No class today Senior defense! **R&C** **SENIOR DEFENSES NO CLASS!**	Bio: **Homework:**<ul><li>Weekly Calendar</li><li>All late work and revisions - **Due Wednesday June 6th at 12pm**</li><li>Begin Benchmark #4 (IAKT): Summary of Evidence (Ultimately, your arrest warrant!)</li><li>Complete <u>Part II: Fingerprinting</u> **ONLY**</li><li>Bio Spring Final is **Wed/Thurs of finals week!** Complete the study guide by hand, and you can use it on the exam!</li></ul> **Objective:** Students will practice determining blood types by using Punnett squares and will continue working on their investigations. **Essential Question:** How can we use the principles of heredity and inheritance to solve a crime?	Bio: **Homework:**<ul><li>Weekly Calendar</li><li>All late work and revisions - **Due Wednesday June 6th at 12pm**</li><li>Begin Benchmark #4 (IAKT): Summary of Evidence (Ultimately, your arrest warrant!)</li><li>Complete <u>Part II: Fingerprinting</u> **ONLY**</li><li>Bio Spring Final is **Wed/Thurs of finals week!** Complete the study guide by hand, and you can use it on the exam!</li></ul> **Objective:** Students will determine the blood type of the blood evidence, will write their next subpoena, and will continue working on their investigations. **Essential Question:** How can we use the principles of heredity and inheritance to solve a crime?

Monday 5/13 (No class)	Tuesday 5/14–Wednesday 5/15 (89-minute blocks)	Thursday 5/16 (44-minute periods)

(Objective:

Students will circle up and pitch their trailer to the class.)

EQ:

What does it take to make a film?

- Have your head writer pitch your team's trailer idea (guiding questions: What is the genre? What music will you use? How will you integrate in the scientific method? When will you meet to film? What resources, materials, etc., do you need to make your trailer?)

Standard: HS.LS3-1, 3-2, 3-3; CCSS.ELA-LITERACY.RST.9-10.4

Agenda:

- Do Now: Agency Log
- With a partner, watch the Blood Types video and complete the notesheet (hard copy)
- Blood-typing Punnett squares practice
- Show all work and complete the exercise on the back of the **Blood Types video notesheet**
- Team document: Punnett squares for suspects
- Investigation board work time
- Suspect list
- Suspect photos
- Prepare for the lab next time! Do this virtual blood-typing lab as our pre-lab
- Blood-typing article (use this article to help you with the pre-lab!)
- Exit ticket: Complete the reflection box of your Agency log

R&C

Objective:

Students will complete Benchmark Two.

EQ:

What does it take to make a film?

- Jump start: Watch *The Shining* or watch *Scary Mary*: How does editing shape meaning? & update Trello board
- Need WeVideo? See me.
- Work time for Benchmark Two: CSI Screenplay, Storyboard, & Moodboard (do this however you want, on the bottom of your organization doc, on a separate doc or slide show or on paper)

Standard: HS.LS3-2, 3-3; CCSS.ELA-LITERACY.RST.9-10.3, 9-10.4, 9-10.7, 9-10.10

Agenda:

- Do Now: Agency Log
- With a partner, watch the Blood Types video and complete the notesheet (hard copy)
- Blood-typing Punnett squares practice
- Show all work and complete the exercise on the back of the **Blood Types video notesheet**
- Team document: Punnett squares for suspects
- Investigation board work time
- Suspect list
- Suspect photos
- Prepare for the lab next time! Do this virtual blood-typing lab as our pre-lab
- Blood-typing article (use this article to help you with the pre-lab!)
- Exit ticket: Complete the reflection box of your Agency log

R&C

Objective:

Students will identify tasks to complete for the CSI trailer and work toward getting them done.

EQ:

What does it take to make a film?

- Jump start: update Trello board
- Work time for Benchmark Three: Rough Cut
- Exit ticket: Update Trello board
- Reminders: Take footage (film & still frames) of labs in biology & link to Organization Doc & link to K/NTKs

(Continued)

(Continued)

Monday 5/13 (No class)	Tuesday 5/14– Wednesday 5/15 (89-minute blocks)	Thursday 5/16 (44-minute periods)
	• **Benchmark Two: CSI Screenplay, Storyboard, & Moodboard DUE** Submit by putting your materials on the Organization Doc) • Exit ticket: Update Trello board & Jolly Questions • Reminders: Take footage (film & still frames) of labs in biology & link to Organization Doc & link to K/NTKs • Filmmaking Resources • Watch one of last year's or the previous year's CSI trailers	• Filmmaking Resources • Watch one of last year's trailers or the previous year's CSI trailers • If you don't have a direct task to do for the CSI trailer, pick one of the following to stay focused: work on biology, do the Deep Dive and make your own blooper reel video, find a video or article about filmmaking need to knows, work on your Professional Portfolio website, practice coding on code. org, if in drivers' ed., complete the final product, play around on WolframAlpha

Monday 5/20	Tuesday 5/21– Wednesday 5/22	Thursday 5/23–Friday 5/24
Bio: **Homework:** • Weekly Calendar • All late work and revisions are **due Wednesday June 6th at 12pm** • Benchmark #2: Fingerprinting Subpoena past due • Bio Spring Final is **Wed/Thurs of finals week!** Complete the study guide by hand, and you can use it on the exam! **Objective:** Students will work on their investigation boards. **Essential Question:** How can we use biology to solve a crime? **Standard:** HS.LS3-1, 3-2, 3-3 **Agenda:** • CSI Awards Pre-party, sign up to bring food or drinks! • Investigation board work time • Suspect list • Suspect photos	Bio: **Homework:** • Weekly Calendar • All late work and revisions - **Due Wednesday June 6th at 12pm** • Benchmark #2: Blood-typing subpoena - **Due Sunday by 11:59 pm** • Bio Spring Final is **Wed/Thurs of finals week!** Complete the study guide by hand, and you can use it on the exam! **Objective:** Students will determine the blood type of the blood evidence, will write their next subpoena, and will continue working on their investigations. **Essential Question:** How can we use the principles of heredity and inheritance to solve a crime? **Standard:** HS.LS3-2, 3-3; CCSS. ELA-LITERACY.RST.9-10.3, 9-10.4, 9-10.7, 9-10.10	Bio: **Homework:** • Weekly Calendar • All late work and revisions are **due Wednesday June 6th at 12pm** • Benchmark #3: Blood-typing subpoena **due today in class!** • Bio Spring Final is **Wed/Thurs of finals week!** Complete the study guide by hand, and you can use it on the exam! **Objective:** Students will determine the blood type of the blood evidence, will write their next subpoena, and will continue working on their investigations. **Essential Question:** How could we sort and predict transfer of hereditary information? **Standard:** HS.LS3-2, 3-3; CCSS. ELA-LITERACY.RST.9-10.3, 9-10.4, 9-10.7, 9-10.10

Monday 5/20	Tuesday 5/21–Wednesday 5/22	Thursday 5/23–Friday 5/24
R&C	**Agenda:**	**Agenda:**

R&C

Objective:

Students will reflect on their ability to collaborate.

EQ:

How does peer feedback improve the quality of our work?

- Pass back all rubrics (How should we use these?)
- Look at collaboration rubric and discuss (What's going well in your team? Challenges?) How will you problem-solve and overcome any setbacks?
- Improve your Professional Portfolio website (use the excellent examples); set a time to meet with me to discuss how you improved your website.

- Check out some amazing Professional Portfolio websites:
  - Example One
  - Example Two
  - Example Three
  - Example Four
  - Example Five
  - Example Six
  - Example Seven
  - Example Eight
  - Example Nine
  - Example Ten

Tuesday 5/21–Wednesday 5/22

Agenda:

- Daily Dose: Agency log and fill out this form
- Blood-typing lab (hard copy)
- Blood-typing article (use this article to help you with the pre-lab!)
- Benchmark #2: Blood-typing subpoena
  - Due Sunday by 11:59 pm
  - Submit here!
- Investigation board work time
- Suspect list
- Suspect photos
- Exit ticket: Complete the reflection box of your Agency log

**Teacher directions for blood-typing lab

R&C

Objective:

Students can revisit norms and reflect on the project so far, as well as work to create a rough cut for their CSI trailer.

EQ:

How do filmmakers use editing techniques to influence our understanding of the story and create audience responses?

- Jump start: Mid-project reflection (team meeting—revisit team contract/norms/roles) What are 3 things going well? What are 3 things that need improvement?
- Filming Norms
- Update Trello
- Work time for Benchmark Three: Trailer Rough Cuts
- Need WeVideo? See me.
- Exit ticket: Update Trello board
- Reminders: Take footage (film & still frames) of labs in biology & Link to Organization Doc & Link to K/NTKs
- Filmmaking Resources

Thursday 5/23–Friday 5/24

Agenda:

- Daily Dose: Agency log and fill out this form
- CSI Awards Pre-Party—sign up to bring food or drinks!
- Blood-typing lab (hard copy)
- Blood-typing article (use this article to help you with the pre-lab!)
- Benchmark #3: Blood-typing subpoena
  - Due today in class!
  - Submit here!
- Investigation board work time
- Suspect list
- Suspect photos
- Exit ticket: Complete the reflection box of your Agency log

**Teacher directions for blood-typing lab

R&C

Objective:

Students can work to create a rough cut for their CSI trailer and get Critical Friends feedback.

EQ:

How does peer feedback improve the quality of our work?

- Jump start: Update Trello board regarding seeking feedback & watch *Austin's Butterfly* to better understand meaningful feedback and its power for achieving high-quality work. What are the qualities of meaningful feedback?
- Explore rubric
- **Benchmark Three: Trailer Rough Cuts DUE**
- Peer Review Trailer Rough Cuts
- Exit ticket: Team meeting to review feedback and update Trello with next steps
- Reminders: Take footage (film & still frames) of labs in biology & link to Organization Doc & link to K/NTKs

(Continued)

(Continued)

Monday 5/20	Tuesday 5/21–Wednesday 5/22	Thursday 5/23–Friday 5/24
	• Learn about Content ID (upload your video to YouTube and make sure it doesn't get taken down) • Watch one of last year's trailers or the previous year's CSI trailers • If you don't have a direct task to do for the CSI trailer, pick one of the following to stay focused: work on biology, do the Deep Dive and make your own blooper reel video, find a video or article about filmmaking need to knows, work on your Professional Portfolio website, practice coding on code.org, if in drivers' ed., complete the final product, play around on WolframAlpha	• Filmmaking Resources • Learn about Content ID (upload your video to YouTube and make sure it doesn't get taken down) • Watch one of last year's trailers or the previous year's CSI trailers • If you don't have a direct task to do for the CSI trailer pick one of the following to stay focused: work on biology, do the Deep Dive and make your own blooper reel video, find a video or article about filmmaking need to knows, work on your Professional Portfolio website, practice coding on code.org, if in drivers' ed., complete the final product, play around on WolframAlpha

Monday 5/27	Tuesday 5/28-Wednesday 5/29	Thursday 5/30-Friday 5/31
NO SCHOOL	Bio: **Homework:** • Weekly Calendar • All late work and revisions are **due Wednesday June 6th at 12pm** • Bring your contribution for the Pre-Party **on Monday**! • Extra credit: Handwritten Cornell notes on article • Folders due **on Thurs/Fri!** • Benchmark #4: PCR/Gel Electrophoresis Subpoena due next class! • Bio Spring Final is **Wed/Thurs of finals week!** Complete the study guide by hand and you can use it on the exam! **Objective:** Students will learn how DNA is analyzed in the lab and will examine the DNA evidence from the crime scene to write their final subpoena. **Essential Question:** How can DNA be analyzed to be used as evidence? **Standard:** HS.LS3-1; CCSS.ELA-LITERACY.RST.9-10.3, 9-10.4, 9-10.10	Bio: **Homework:** • Weekly Calendar • All late work and revisions are _due Wednesday June 6th at 12pm_ • Bring your contribution for the Pre-Party **on Monday!** • Extra credit: Handwritten Cornell notes on article • Benchmark #4: PCR/Gel Electrophoresis Subpoena due today in class! • Folders due **today!** • Informal presentations as your final **next class!** • Bio Spring Final is **Wed/Thurs of finals week!** Complete the study guide by hand and you can use it on the exam! **Objective:** Students will complete their final subpoena, will submit their arrest warrant, and will wrap up pending assignments. **Essential Question:** How can DNA be analyzed to be used as evidence? **Standard:** HS.LS3-1; CCSS.ELA-LITERACY.RST.9-10.7

Monday 5/27	Tuesday 5/28–Wednesday 5/29	Thursday 5/30–Friday 5/31
	Agenda:	**Agenda:**

Tuesday 5/28–Wednesday 5/29

Agenda:

- Daily Dose: Agency log
- Review DNA PPT, take Cornell notes
- Electrophoresis online lab
- Release Gels results
- Benchmark #4: PCR/Gel Electrophoresis Subpoena
- Submit here!
- Investigation board work time
- Suspect list
- Suspect photos
- Exit ticket: Complete the reflection box of your Agency log

R&C

Objective:

Students can use the CF feedback they received on their rough cuts to edit the final cut of their CSI trailer.

EQ:

How do filmmakers use editing techniques to influence our understanding of the story and create audience responses?

- *Final CSI Trailer Due 5/29*
- Jump start: Update Trello board & re-read Project Guidelines & rubric & update K/NTKs
- Work time: Final Cut
- Exit ticket: Update Trello board
- Reminders: Take footage (film & still frames) of labs in biology & link to Organization Doc & link to K/NTKs
- Filmmaking Resources
- Learn about Content ID (upload your video to YouTube and make sure it doesn't get taken down)
- Watch one of last year's trailers or the previous year's CSI trailers
- If you don't have a direct task to do for the CSI trailer, pick one of the following to stay focused: work on biology, do the Deep Dive and make your own blooper reel video, find a video or article about filmmaking need to knows, work on your Professional Portfolio website, practice coding on code.org, if in drivers' ed., complete the final product, play around on WolframAlpha

Thursday 5/30–Friday 5/31

Agenda:

- Daily Dose: Agency log
- Submit Arrest warrant (one per team or you will be disqualified!)
- Review your contribution for the Pre-Party and bring it on Monday!
- Turn in folders
- Finish and submit Benchmark #4: PCR/Gel Electrophoresis Subpoena
- Submit here!
- Finish investigation boards
- Suspect list
- Suspect photos
- If time, begin Collaboration Reflection
- If time, extra credit: handwritten Cornell notes on article
- Complete the reflection box of your Agency log
- Submit your Agency Log here!

R&C

Objective:

Students can practice collaboration and reflect on their individual and team collaboration.

EQ:

How does reflection improve the quality of my work?

- Jump start: Finalize Trello board make sure it's shared with me and updated to reflect the finished project
- Work time: CSI Project Reflection (print out)
- Pass back WHO ARE YOU? from beginning of year (how have you stayed the same, changed?)
- Collaboration Scenarios
- Watch CSI Videos
- Reminders: Link to Organization Doc

*All late work and revisions are *due Wednesday June 6th at 3pm**

(Continued)

(Continued)

Monday 6/3	Tuesday 6/4	Wednesday 6/5	Thursday 6/6	Friday 6/7
Awards Show during 2-7 ● Bio Spring Final is **Wed/Thurs of finals week!** Complete the study guide by hand, and you can use it on the exam!	Bio: **Homework:** ● Presenting Investigation Boards **today!** ● Submit Collab Peer Feedback **today!** ● Extra credit: Handwritten Cornell notes on article **due Wednesday June 6th at 12pm** ● All late work and revisions are due Wednesday June 6th at 12pm Bio Spring Final is **Wed/Thurs this week!** Complete the study guide by hand, and you can use it on the exam! **Objective:** Students will present their investigation boards and will reflect on their teammates' collaboration. **Essential Question:** How can we use biology to solve a crime? **Standard:** HS.LS3-1, 3-2, 3-3; CCSS.ELA-LITERACY.RST.9-10.7 **Agenda:** ● Daily Dose: None ● Present investigation boards (rubric here) ● Clean out team drawers ● Collaboration Peer Feedback ● Project Debrief	Bio: **Homework:** ● Presenting Investigation Boards **today!** ● Submit Collab Peer Feedback **today!** ● Extra credit: Handwritten Cornell notes on article **due today at 12pm** ● All late work and revisions are due today at 12pm Bio Spring Final is **Wed/Thurs this week!** Complete the study guide by hand, and you can use it on the exam! **Objective:** Students will present their investigation boards and will reflect on their teammates' collaboration. **Essential Question:** How can we use biology to solve a crime? **Standard:** HS.LS3-1, 3-2, 3-3; CCSS.ELA-LITERACY.RST.9-10.7 **Agenda:** ● Daily Dose: None ● Present investigation boards (rubric here) ● Clean out team drawers ● Collaboration Peer Feedback ● Project Debrief	Bio: **Homework:** ● None **Objective:** Students will debrief the project and end the year with affirmations. **Essential Question:** How can we end the year on a high note? **Agenda:** ● Daily Dose: None ● Project debrief ● Affirmations	**Last Day of School! Minimum Day** 1st: 7:45–8:25 Advisory and Summer Feast: 8:30–11:45 Senior Graduation Practice 8:00 am–9:00 am *Dismissal at 11:45 am*

•FIGURE 8.4 **Blank Project Calendar**

Use this calendar to plan out your project benchmarks. Remember, this is just big-picture planning—don't worry yet about your everyday lessons.

CraftED Project Calendar

Topics/Themes Benchmarks	Monday	Tuesday	Wednesday	Thursday	Friday
Week 1					
Week 2					
Week 3					
Week 4					
Week 5					
Week 6					
Week 7					
Week 8					

Source: ©2018 Jennifer Piearatt.

Download this template at resources.corwin.com/keepitrealPBLsecondary

Hear from secondary teachers about how they use the calendaring process in their project plans:

Calendaring has become essential to my project planning. Charting daily work to driving questions from projects in my science and math classes has allowed me to connect meaning to daily tasks. I think students can find relevance when they see that skill building work is part of product development and has a clear progression to add to what is exhibited and curated. My most successful projects have come when project stakeholders such as students, support staff, and collaborators have given input throughout the process to ensure content, timing, and pacing are appropriate.

—Mathew Leader, High School Math and
Science Teacher, High Tech High/Middle North County

Calendaring out a project is extremely helpful for me within the co-planning process because it helps me to see how I can blend the standards and project seamlessly within the timeframe desired, and that always helps me breathe easier. Calendaring projects also ensures the meaningfulness and relevance of the content being taught, and that is critical to my math classroom.

—Brooke Tobia, Middle School Math Teacher,
Calavera Hill Middle School

As an inclusion specialist, co-planning [through the calendaring process] with teachers on projects was imperative. We would look at the final product and backward plan to determine what pieces of a project we would expect to be challenging for our special education students. Ultimately, we focused on the overall purpose of the project. What did we want students to learn from this experience? We found ways in which to include these students in the project that incorporated their strengths and allowed for them to come out of the project with content knowledge and skill development.

—Andy Krauthoefer, Former High School
Teacher and Inclusion Specialist, High Tech High North County

Getting help with the process of calendaring is one of the most crucial components in the creation of any PBL unit, as it allows me to envision the unit as a whole while also looking at the breakdown of tasks and assessments. Being able to make connections between the driving question, the standards, the tasks, and the assessments is key in planning PBL units, and calendaring is the cornerstone that allows that to happen.

—Penny Barachkov, Middle School Humanities Teacher,
Aviara Oaks Middle School

Differentiating Project Plans

As you continue to keep drilling down into your project plans, you will want to begin to think about differentiation—will different students need different paths to get to project milestones? What additional resources or support will be needed within each of the phases and days you are planning? Use the differentiation checklist provided in Figure 8.5 to help you think through your plans for differentiating instruction within your project.

Tip for planning for differentiation:
On my project calendars, I used to note
the following for each day's plans:

1.  Mild option: for students who may need additional resources, support, or reteach lessons and activities.

2. Medium option: activities for students who were right on pace.

3. Spicy option: challenge options for student who were ready to dive a little deeper into project work.

Source: Mild option malerpaso/iStock .com. Medium option deepblue4you/ iStock.com. Spicy option dreamnikon/iStock.com.

● **FIGURE 8.5** Differentiation Checklist for Project Planning

PBL on Demand
Project Differentiation Checklist

© CraftED Curriculum LLC

PROJECT PLANNING

☐ Define options for final products (Remember: same skills and content!)

☐ Alter benchmark process and deliverables, as needed

☐ Identify, prepare, collect scaffolds for ALL

☐ Create daily lesson plans with low, medium, and high levels in mind

☐ Connect with Inclusion Teacher, plan for coteaching if needed

PROJECT LAUNCH

☐ Share learning goals/success criteria, assessment expectations

☐ Conduct preassessment

☐ Collect need to knows, alter plans as needed

☐ RAFT, Challenge options welcome   ☐ Project groups, contracts

DURING THE PROJECT

☐ Run workshops, individual conferencing on benchmarks

☐ Include (informal) daily checks for understanding, adapt as needed

☐ Assess benchmark deliverables, provide feedback group, reteach, or challenge as needed

☐ Create a transparent and reflective classroom culture: mild, medium, spicy

Does your school have an inclusion model?
Are you wondering how that model works with PBL?
Here are commonly asked questions with #realtalk
answers to help you in you in your PBL journey.

Inclusion in PBL: Frequently Asked Questions

Q1: Can all kids really do PBL? What about kids with IEPs?

A1: The short answer is YES! When I was a teacher at High Tech High, one of the design principles was "a common intellectual mission," which meant that our classrooms were fully inclusive of all learners. Our founder, Larry Rosenstock, used to preach about the beauty of PBL in helping to operationalize this Design Principle because it allowed us to "set the floor and open the ceiling." PBL provides an open-ended framework that allows students to experience the learning process very differently, if need be. The scaffolds that are critical to PBL are good for *all* students, not just those with special needs.

Q2: At what point should I involve inclusion teachers in my project plans?

A2: Here are some entry points for when you can bring inclusion teachers into your project plans:

- Involve them in the early stages of brainstorming, once you have landed on your EU, DQ, final product, and culminating experience. They may be able to tell you in these early stages what hurdles you may need to address for some students.

- When you are designing your assessment tools, it is helpful to have inclusion teachers work alongside you so that you can talk about how you will need to "alter the path" for certain students.

- When calendaring your project, inclusion teachers may be able to create separate calendars for students with IEPs who need smaller benchmarks to help them stay organized.

(Continued)

(Continued)

- Do weekly check-ins on IEP student progress with project benchmarks. This allows inclusion teachers to front-load content or skills if needed and ensure that students with special needs don't fall behind.
- Include them during daily lesson planning so material can be modified or created in a variety of formats for diverse learning needs/styles.

Q3: What is the best way to work with an inclusion teacher that "pushes into my classroom"?

A3: Having an extra set of hands is a blessing! Here are some ways you and an inclusion teacher can work together to support students during the course of a project:

- During project work time: This time can often be hard for students with special needs to stay on task.
- During group work: If students need social skills support, it is helpful to have an inclusion teacher present to help you support all students.
- To coteach a lesson or run a small workshop: I repeat—extra hands are a blessing!

Q4: What does coteaching look like in PBL?

A4: Think of coteaching like a "tag-team" with your favorite superhero! Each of you can teach to your strengths, and that benefits *everybody*! You can group students according to learning styles and needs, and each of you can take a group to run a small workshop. These groups don't have to be separated by IEP or 504 students; you can do heterogeneous grouping that all students will benefit from!

Q5: Where can I learn more about inclusion in PBL?

A5: This isn't a topic that is covered often, so it's hard to find good content on this topic. But here are a few of my favorite resources:

- Visit the companion website (resources.corwin.com/keepitrealPBLsecondary) to find links to two blog posts:
  - "How to Run a Student-Led IEP in a PBL Setting"
  - "All About Inclusion in PBL via PBLWorks Blog"
- *Project Based Teaching* by Boss and Larmer, 2018
- Follow my favorite PBL inclusion teacher on social media: Kristin Uliasz, @MsUliasz

As you think about your project plans, how might you need to make adjustments to meet the needs of all students in your classroom?

Chapter 9
Classroom Management in PBL

Managing the project process is critical, especially when working with younger students. In the following pages are four management strategies to help provide structure to the project experience. Despite the common misconception that PBL is open-ended and/or student-driven, the teacher definitely plays a hefty role in establishing structures, routines, and protocols to help collaboratively manage project work (see Figure 9.1).

Photo courtesy of Chris Nelson Photography.

● **FIGURE 9.1** Jenny and Lake Elementary teachers analyzing student work during a reflective exercise

Establish a Central Location for Project Resources

Identify some wall space in your classroom that can be dedicated to important project related items (see Figure 9.2). You will want to physically post these items:

- One-page overview of the project (for examples, check out Appendix A and the companion website—resources.corwin.com/keepitrealPBLsecondary)
- Know/Need to know chart (more on this in Chapter 10)
- Project calendar
- Graphic organizers or handouts for project benchmarks
- Project rubric
- Field work contact information
- Group contracts

● **FIGURE 9.2** Project wall from the classroom of Jen Stillittano of Central Coast New Tech

It is also recommended to have project resources be digital, via a "project hub." By going digital, students can build their agency by having more access to information and responsibility to store project resources and work. Check out the companion website (resources.corwin.com/keepitrealPBLsecondary) for two examples of project hubs.

Make the Project Process Visible

Tracking groups throughout the project process can get a little overwhelming as the project unfolds, and some groups move ahead, while others fall behind. It is important to track where groups are within the project both for your sanity and for students' ownership of their learning. One way you can visibly see where project groups are in the process of a project is through clip charts (see Figure 9.3). You can create a chart using butcher paper to laterally list out the project benchmarks, or even break those benchmarks further with daily assignments in a week. From there, each group gets a clothespin with their names on it. Either the teacher can move these or students can as they progress through the phases of the project.

Another method for making the project process visible is the Scrum board (see Figure 9.4), which comes from professional industries grounded in innovation and design. To make a Scrum board, you can simply use blue painter's tape to create a table with column headers at the top of project benchmarks and rows titled with individual tasks within a benchmark. Each group or individual student then has a sticky note with their name(s) on it, which moves along as they progress through project tasks.

Want to learn more about the Scrum process in your classroom? Check out the companion website (resources.corwin.com/keepitrealPBLsecondary) for more information.

● **FIGURE 9.3** Sample Project Clip Chart

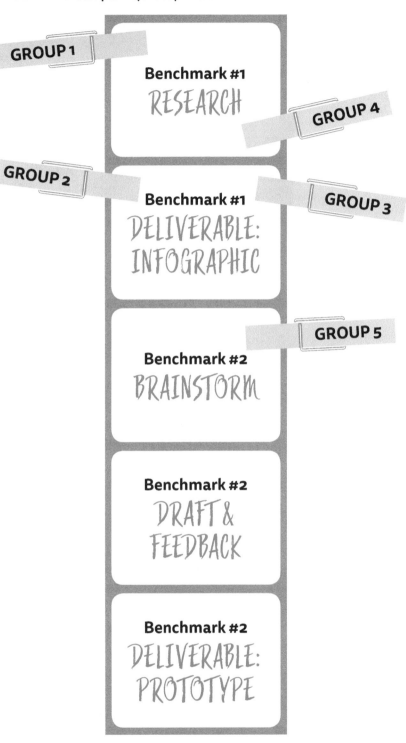

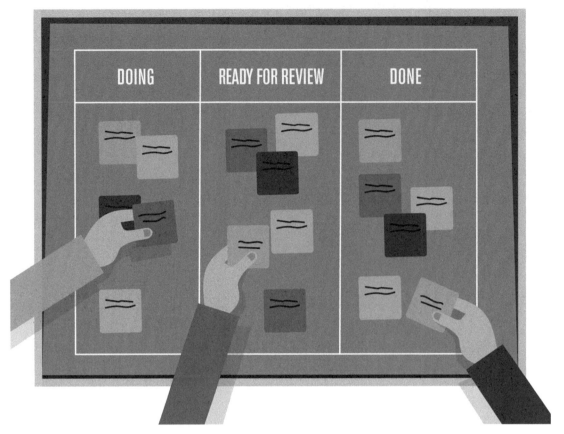

danijela1a/iStock.com

● **FIGURE 9.4** Process-oriented project Scrum board. Notice how the board keeps track of what students are *Doing*, what they have *Ready for Review*, and what they have *Done*.

Use Group Contracts, Protocols, and Roles

Before you go any further down the collaboration crosswalk, be sure that the project task is truly one that requires collaboration. Use Figure 9.5 to help you conduct a reality check before you even place students into groups.

If you decide that the project work truly necessitates collaboration, here are a few tips to help you manage group work.

Group contracts (see Figure 9.6) serve as an agreement between group members for how they will behave within their project group. Group contracts align with the responsive classroom approach to norming, or traditional social contracts established at the beginning of the year. The use of the contract is integral in continuing to build student agency by putting the ownership on students to work together productively and to hold one another accountable for their project work.

Jen Stillittano of Central Coast New Tech tailors her group contract process according to the requirements of each project and provides an example from a ninth-grade project on designing a digital portfolio.

●FIGURE 9.5 Crafting Collaboration Reality Check

Crafting Collaboration

via CraftED Curriculum

Start with some critical reality checks

REALITY CHECK 1

Is this a task students could complete on their own? Do they NEED each other to learn more deeply?

REALITY CHECK 2

Do all students have the necessary background knowledge to enter into the task?

REALITY CHECK 4

Does this task ensure equal thinking, not just equal doing?

REALITY CHECK 3

Is the task open-ended so all group members can continue to contribute?

REALITY CHECK 5

What issues of status do you need to be mindful of with this task?

REALITY CHECK 6

What types of (differentiated) scaffolds might you need?

START PLANNING

For more teaching materials visit

www.craftedcurriculum.com

(Continued)

● FIGURE 9.5 (Continued)

Build the structures for success

STATE THE EXPECTATION

How will you assess? What do you want students to learn/do? You may even co-construct this with students.

*check our strategy "Co-constructing DL Assessments"

DEVELOP NORMS

And revisit them often through meaningful reflections and feedback.

HAVE A GAME PLAN

What steps will students take every day? To start? When stuck? When finished? Build those agency muscles!

SCHEDULE CHECK-INS

Conference with groups daily and 1:1 when needed. Perhaps have a noted schedule. Maybe "call the coach" for when you are needed on demand.

HAVE A PROTOCOL

What happens when groups have problems? How do you work through the challenges?

*check out our "problem-solving protocol"

BE READY TO DIFFERENTIATE

What skills will some students need, but not others? What workshops can you offer?

PROVIDE ONGOING FEEDBACK AND ASSESSMENT

Come back to those expectations. Have students reflect and offer feedback often. Consider: group, self, teacher, formative, summative.

DEEPER LEARNING FOR ALL STUDENTS

Self-Contract and Task Management

You must create a contract that will serve as the guiding document for your personal and collaborative behavior and task completion. This document should explain the various methods and tools you have chosen to use to manage your time and tasks that you need to complete in life, both academically and socially. Explain why you have chosen these techniques and how you will use them to monitor and manage the tasks you will need to complete for your professional digital portfolio. Follow this example:

> "I use my Google Calendar and have it synced among all of my devices. I often set up alerts and plan out my schedule at the beginning of each week. I have chosen Google Calendar because it's free, it syncs among my devices, and, most importantly, this method helps me keep the commitments I make to both myself and others. To guide the work I need to do for my portfolio, I will use my Google Calendar as a place to identify when and what I specifically need to get done."

Final contracts and task calendars must be approved by the teacher and shared with your advisor.

Instructions: Please make a copy of this document and submit by copying and pasting a **hyperlink** to the submission box in Echo.

1. Learn about the elements of a SMART (specific, measurable, attainable, relevant, and timely) goal by watching the videos and reading the articles provided.

   - Copy and paste your SMART goal into the notes section of your Table of Contents!
     - My SMART goal for second semester is . . .

2. List positive qualities you want others to notice in you in this semester.

3. Describe your vision of success; how has it grown and developed since last semester? You must use at least five of the following words in your vision of success:

   - Realization
   - Gamut
   - Security
   - Achievement
   - Excess
   - Integrity
   - Humility
   - Intuition
   - Procrastination
   - Rational
   - Interchangeable
   - Vision
   - Elaborate
     - My vision of success is . . .

(Continued)

(Continued)

4. List criteria on the [New Tech Network] Agency rubric that you want to work on this semester.

   ● List specific items on the Agency rubric you want to work on this semester.

5. Explain the various methods and tools you have chosen to use to manage your time and tasks that you need to complete in life, both academically and socially; explain why you have chosen these techniques and how you will use them to monitor and manage the tasks you will need to complete for your professional portfolio:

There are a variety of ready-made group contracts you can use; check out a few on the companion website (resources.corwin.com/ keepitrealPBLsecondary).

There is no right way to form project groups. Different projects can allow for different grouping strategies. Perhaps students are grouped by research questions or interest or maybe by final product options. Sometimes, this will mean that students are grouped homogeneously, and other times, it may be that they are in heterogeneous groups.

There are many protocols for group work, but my favorites are included in a resource by Expeditionary Learning, accessible on the companion website (resources.corwin.com/ keepitrealPBLsecondary).

Regardless of which format you use for your group contract, it is critical that you keep this document alive. Ask students to pull out their contracts each day to generate goals or reflect upon their collaboration.

Another structure you can put in place to allow for equitable contributions and increased student agency within a group is the use of protocols. Protocols ensure that all students have the opportunity to participate and also serve as a great way to scaffold collaboration by teaching students how to listen, engage in discourse, and/or provide feedback to one another.

Role cards can be another helpful structure for ensuring that all group members are contributing; however, you want to be careful that roles are leading to equal thinking, not just equal doing. Traditionally, roles such as scribes or material collectors can escape from having to do any heavy lifting in the project, leaving the critical thinking to fall on the shoulders of one student. I've provided some sample role cards for Grades 6–8 (Figure 9.7) and Grades 9–12 (Figure 9.8) that you can copy and cut out if you'd like. If you chose to use group role cards, be sure that each group member's tasks are equitable to the project work and consider providing them with sentence frames to help scaffold their contributions to the group.

● FIGURE 9.6 Group Game Plan for Project Work Time Management

CraftED

Group Game Plan

Project:

Group Assignment:

Names	Contact Information
1.	
2.	
3.	
4.	
5.	

As a group, we hope to . . .

A strength each person brings to this group is . . .

A worry or fear each person has about working together/this project is . . .

Some challenges we may face during this project are . . .

If we run into these challenges, we will . . .

We will make decisions by . . .

As a group, we agree to . . .

If a group member is not upholding this game plan, as a group we will . . .

Student Name	Signature	Parent	Teacher

Source: ©2018 Jennifer Piearatt

 Download this template at resources.corwin.com/keepitrealPBLsecondary

● FIGURE 9.7 Grades 6–8 Role Cards

Connections King

Discourse Diva

Quality Control

Mindset Maven

Help your peers to make connections between what you are
learning about and the real world; this can include
things happening in your community, on the news, or things
you have learned about before.

Sentence frames:
"Does what we are talking about remind anybody of _____?"
"How does this relate to something we have learned about?"
"Your idea sounds a lot like _____."

Help your peers to be mindful of their language. This relates to how your group members
interact—remind them to "share the air", listen to others' perspectives, and work together
by learning from one another. You can also help them to bring in vocabulary from what you
are learning about as part of your conversations.

Sentence frames:
" _____ (group member name) had a great idea, _____ (other group member name)
can you build off of his/her idea?"
" _____ (group member name)
you raise a great point, can somebody give
us a new perspective/idea on this?"
" _____ (group member name)) the
idea that you just gave us sounds a lot like _____ (content vocabulary), would you agree?"

Ensure that your group is using tools and techniques from the content area you
are studying. You also want to encourage your group to produce the highest quality of work possible.

Sentence frames:
"We can help each other make our work the very
best by _____."
"A tool that we should be using today during work time is _____; some ways
that we can use that tool are _____."
"A formula/resource that could be helpful for us is _____."

Your job is to help remind your group members to be reflective and mindful of
the energy of your group. You can do this by using positive language, paying attention to the
behavior of group members, and offering reminders.

Sentence frames:
"Some challenges today were _____; how did we respond?"
"What is something we want to celebrate about how our group worked together?
What is something we can improve next time we work together?"
"If the vibe of our group had a color today. it would be _____ because _____."

● **FIGURE 9.8** Grades 9–12 Role Cards

Subject Matter Expert (SME)

Pre-Trouble Shooter

Collaboration Climatologist

Meta Master

As the SME you need to help your group by ensuring that you are connecting your ideas and conversations to core content. You can do this by reminding your peers to use content vocabulary, or helping your group to draw connections between
procedures /theories /themes /equations that you have learned in class and the real world.

Sentence starters:
"One connection that we can make between our group conversation and what we have learned during this unit is _____ ."

"The idea that our group is coming up with sounds a lot like _____ that we just learned about."

Your task is to identify potential problems your group may face and help your group address them. You can facilitate this process by ensuring action steps for all group members are clear, help to identify potential roadblocks your group may face, along with resources and appropriate tools.

Sentence starters:
"A challenge we will likely face with this task is _____ ; therefore we should be ready to _____ ."
"In case we get stuck with /by _____ , then we should all practice agency by using the following resources _____ ."

Your role is to monitor the climate of your group work. You can do this by tracking group goals, ensure all voices and perspectives are considered, facilitate peer feedback and revision for work completed during this unit/project.

Sentence starters:
"Our group identify _____ as a goal; How do you each feel we are doing with this goal?"

"Our group is considering doing _____ , how do all members feel about this?"

"We can improve our work if we work together—let's take some time to stop and give somebody in our group feedback on their work by doing _____ ."

Your role is to lead your group through the process of being reflective learners. You can do this by helping your group celebrate success and failure, encourage peers who are struggling with a fixed mindset, help the group to make decisions based on developing individuals' strengths and areas for growth.

Sentence starters:
"As our group worked together today I saw _____ really challenge himself /herself by _____ ."

"What is one way our group can help each individual in this group grow as learner?"

"I saw _____ 'fail forward' this week by doing _____ .
Did anybody else see /experience something like that this week?"

If you have an inclusion model at your school, consider working together with your inclusion staff to support your classroom management efforts to help with the project process for *all* students.

Behavior is communication. We often see students acting out if they are feeling lost, confused, or disconnected from the classroom. We worked tirelessly to ensure that students were accessing the classroom in a way that met their needs through collaboration and preplanning. As an inclusion specialist, I worked with teachers to develop specific tasks and roles within the context of projects that empowered our students with learning differences to contribute and thrive, giving them a sense of purpose and connection to the class. When students were engaged and felt they had a purpose, the difficult behavior subsided, allowing inclusion staff the ability to focus on academics and skill development in the classroom, not through pull out.

—Andrew Krauthoefer, Former Inclusion Specialist at High Tech High/Current School and Private Practice Counselor, Trailhead Counseling and Wellness, LLC

Consider the Workshop Method

Similar to the writing or reading workshop model by Lucy Calkins used in elementary schools, you may consider using the workshop model for project work. The workshop method provides an embedded opportunity for differentiation in that you can provide diverse levels of minilessons and also pull groups to reteach content or further challenge students. In secondary classrooms implementing PBL, the workshop method looks like this:

- First, a brief minilesson for the whole class, as it relates to project content.
- Next, project work time for students to apply/practice what was learned in the minilesson. The teacher may or may not ask students to create a goal for their work time.
- Then, the teacher conferences with individual students or project groups. During this time, the teacher can provide formative feedback for students or check on group progress.
- Finally, project work time reflection as a closing for the block of time. Students can self-reflect on their progress and generate next steps for the following day. This is also a great time to bring the class back to the K/NTK chart (see Chapter 10).

Check the companion website (resources.corwin.com/keepit realPBLsecondary) for a great resource for seeing the workshop model in action in a primary grade.

#realtalk: There is a fine line between the sound of a healthy project buzz and chaos. Structure is OK in PBL—without it, project work time can lead to anarchy!

What is one management strategy you want to try in your first project? Journal here:

Chapter 10

Launching Your Project

Remember back in your teacher credentialing program when you first learned how to write a lesson plan and it had to start with an anticipatory set? Well, in PBL the project launch, sometimes referred to as "the Entry Event," is the anticipatory set amplified! Launching your project is an opportunity to get students excited about the learning ahead, engage them in inquiry, and also establish some important routines and structures for the work ahead. Project launches live on a spectrum of authenticity and engagement—some are much more complex than others. However, the ultimate goal of your launch is to pique student interest and share expectations for the PBL journey you and your students are embarking upon.

The Hook

The hook is students' first introduction to the project, so we want it to be something that gets them excited about the content they will be learning. Here are some ideas for "hooks," presented in order of preparation required by the teacher (low to high):

- Multimedia: You can show students video clips, TED Talks, satellite images from Google Earth, movie trailers, videos you have recorded, or even a song.
- Simulations, skits, or even pranks: One year as an introduction to learning about Enlightenment philosophers, I set up a prank for my class (with advance parent and administrator notification, of course). I hid a camera in my classroom and stepped out of the room for five minutes during class. Once students realized there was no adult in the room, complete chaos broke out—students were out of their seats, throwing paper and yelling. The following day, students walked into class as the video footage was projected on the board with the driving question: "In the absence of authority, are humans good or bad?" We answered through a Socratic Seminar that segued into the introduction of our project on the ideals behind the American Revolution.
- Guest speakers: You can bring in an expert to present a local problem to students— perhaps your superintendent or a local government official. Guest speakers provide an immediate authentic connection to what students are going to be learning about in the real world. If you can't physically bring in a guest speaker, you can video conference them

in and project them on your screen or have them record a short video and send it to you for you to play for your class during the launch.

● Field work: Taking students out of the classroom is an incredible way to get students excited about an upcoming project. You can do a walking or driving field trip to collect data, see a play or a show, or visit a local attraction or center in your community. If you go this route, be sure to prepare students in advance and don't send them empty-handed; have them document what they see, hear, and think and come back to this to debrief as a class.

The Question Formulation Technique is a great way to launch student inquiry. The following is an excerpt from a post I wrote for the Right Question Institute (www.rightquestion.org; Pieratt, 2019); the remainder of the article can be accessed on the companion website:

A bedrock of high quality PBL is authenticity. One way to achieve real-world connections is through field work. Field work is different from field trips in that students are actively engaged as scientists collecting data and asking questions of what they observe and experience in the field. The newly acquired knowledge and perspective gained through field work can inform student inquiry. Therefore, field work felt like a natural entry point for marrying PBL with the QFT.

This marriage can occur in the project launch phase. Students can hear from a guest speaker (in person or virtually) or visit a community location (physically or virtually) to serve as a focus to the QFT. In this way the initial field work is used as the springboard for the QFT; in other words, "Now that you've learned from your experience, let's use that as the QFocus and ask some questions." A best practice of field work is for students to document and then debrief their learning. The next steps of the QFT can then be used to inform students' initial questions about the project in the next phase of the project launch.

Figures 10.1 and 10.2 also provide sample methods for launching your project.

The Question Formulation Technique (QFT) is a five-step process to facilitate with students to help them generate thoughtful questions to drive their learning. According to the Right Question Institute, the QFT includes the following steps:

1. Introduce/revisit rules, "question focus," and produce questions.

2. Students number and improve their questions.

3. Categorize questions by closed or open-ended, and discuss the value of these types of questions.

4. Change and prioritize questions.

5. Generate next steps based on refined questions.

FIGURE 10.1 Sample Project Launch for Sixth-Grade Humanities Project

Phase	Teacher Moves	Student Actions, Outcomes
1: Simulation	The teacher explains that today we are going to be engaging in a simulation, and although it may feel as if we are talking about a *long* time ago, maybe we will begin to see some connections to us today. The teacher may use one of the following simulations or any other of his or her choosing: Option 1 Option 2 (included in Google folder "Survivor") Option 3	Students participate in simulation to excite them about the content of this project.
2: Debrief	Teacher will pose the following questions to the class for a whole-group discussion: • What did you notice about your behavior? Others' behavior? • What surprised you? • What does this remind you of? • How is it same/different from the ways in which we behave/respond today? *Teacher may choose to do this as a "Think/Pair/Share" or an in-depth Socratic Seminar.	Students will verbally make the connections between ancient human behaviors and current human behaviors/adaptations to living in their surroundings.
3: Intro to project	Teacher will pass out student project overview sheets. Teacher says, "Let's look at a few models of the kind of work you will be engaging in during this project." Teacher will show chosen models of final products (photo essays, 2 voice poetry, letters to government representatives) and ask students to journal and then discuss the visible thinking routine "See, Think, Wonder."	Students will review project sheet using popcorn reading strategy in small groups. Students will analyze exemplar models to inform their "north star" for this project and help initiate questions for N/NTK process next.
4: K/NTKs	Teacher will provide students with five sticky notes and ask them to write down what they know about the project and what they think they need to know. Then, place sticky notes on appropriate place on class T-chart. Teacher should remind students to write their names on the sticky notes. After students have completed this exercise, teacher should categorize and prioritize students NTKs for future workshops.	Students will be able to articulate what they know about this project (content and skills) and what they need to know, in order to drive their learning by engaging in the K/NTK process.
Exit ticket	Teacher shows *Golden Circle* video or *Walking With Purpose* video (search YouTube) to students and then asks them to complete the Golden Circle diagram on the project sheet.	Students complete the exit ticket for teacher approval but keep the form for their reference and parent signature.

● **FIGURE 10.2** **Sample Entry Document for 12th-Grade AP Government Project**

Hello South Putnam students,

At the Center on Representative Government, we believe that it is essential for our citizens to be active participants in the democratic process. In fact, our mission is to help prepare the next generation of citizens by working with educators to create programs that inform, inspire, and motivate students and to encourage civic participation to seek solutions to the many challenges that confront our nation today.

One of the challenges that we have seen rise to the front of our political discussions both nationally and internationally is the refugee crisis. Many people have strong opinions on whether or not our nation should be welcoming to refugees. We would like for you to put aside the opinions about where the refugees should be fleeing to and focus on the places they are fleeing from.

In the top refugee-producing countries, the governments have largely created the situations that force their citizens to leave. It is obvious that, like Iraq and others before them, these nations need a better way of governing their people. We would like for you to create a proposal that describes what type of government would best prevent these crises from happening in the future.

Our goal is to have one of our advisors come to your class to give feedback on your proposals. We will be in touch concerning the date of that event, but we anticipate that it will take about one month to prepare your proposals.

Sincerely,

The Center on Representative Government

Indiana University, Bloomington, IN

Tip: You can ask students to underline what they know and circle what they need to know to help increase participation in the next step of your project launch.

Project Guidelines

Now is the time to pass out your one-page overview that we discussed in the last chapter and read it together or ask students to silently read it using active-reading strategies. This is also the time when you may briefly share with older students the assessment tool and project calendar. For younger students, you can reference important milestones— for example, "We will be working on this project to share it at our open house with our community." Another sample is found in Figure 10.3.

● **FIGURE 10.3** **Sample Project Guidelines for Sixth-Grade Humanities Project**

"The Human Experience: Past to Present"

Student Project Overview

Driving Question: *What is the human experience of adapting to life? How are the current challenges of those living in San Francisco similar and different to those faced by early humans?*

Why: As humans, we tend to naturally categorize and isolate ourselves by finding the many ways in which we are different; however, history, specifically early humans, will show us that we are more alike than we are different— how we adapt, how we migrate, and how we fill our needs. History can also help us better understand, appreciate, and improve the world around us with laws, behaviors, systems, and structures. With this knowledge, we become empowered and possess the ability to be advocates for change in our community.

How: We are going to learn a lot during this project—from the Paleolithic era to the agricultural revolution, to writing, to effectively speaking, to creative uses of technology, to curating our work, and to advocating for our community. We will engage in field work, speak to community members, participate in writing workshops and class discussions, work with our peers, and think deeply and passionately. We will provide each other feedback to develop our very best work that will be shared with a public audience.

What: We will be using technology to research, make infographics, record 2 voice poetry, and document human experiences through photography. We will learn how to write a professional letter to a government official and how to tell a human story through narrative writing and photo essays.

Figure 10.4 is a combination of both a launch activity and a project overview sheet from a 12th-grade AP government project.

● **FIGURE 10.4** **Sample Launch, Hook, and Project Overview**

NOTICE OF VACANCY: District 44, House of Representatives, Indiana

"State Senator, State Representative, Prosecuting Attorney, Circuit Court Clerk, County, City, Town and Township Elective Offices, Town Judges and Township Small Claims Court Judges: All Democratic or Republican Vacancies: These vacancies in elective office are filled by a caucus of the district precinct committeemen affiliated with the political party that elected the candidate who vacated the office." (IC 3-13-5 and IC 3-13-11)

The state of Indiana is looking for candidates to participate in an emergency election on May 3 to serve the remainder of the term of office for District 44. *Normally* (as dictated in the Indiana Constitution), there would be a candidate filled by the party of the person who has left office; however, in this very unusual case the vacancy is caused by an independent candidate who has chosen to take a position in the private sector. Candidates for office need to have prepared a stump speech for May 1 and 2 rallies with the precinct committee members.

Election will be held at South Putnam High School, and candidates will be able to begin their campaigns on April 14.

From now until the election, prepare the following:

1. A political party for your candidate to run under, which includes:

    a. Party name
    b. Party symbol
    c. Party slogan
    d. Candidate for office

        i.   You will make up fake credentials for this person and their career.
        ii. Create a demographic profile that fits your ideal candidate.

    e. Platform

        i.   This must include your party's stance on the key issues facing Indiana.
        ii.   Model it after the major current party political platforms.
        iii. Explain the history of your party: From where do you get your foundations or key beliefs?

(Continued)

● **FIGURE 10.4 (Continued)**

2. Political campaign materials

    a. Posters/ Infographics—*both* digital and physical
    b. Website

        i.   Outlines the candidate's qualifications
        ii.   Outlines the party platform
        iii. Explains where the party falls on the political spectrum

3. Campaign plan

    a. Who is your target demographic?
    b. How will you fund your campaign?
    c. Who will endorse your campaign?
    d. How will you get the word out about your candidate?

4. Stump speech

    a. This will be delivered to the electorate on May 1 and 2 and should persuade the people to vote for your candidate.

Organize all of the evidence of this into a PowerPoint that you will present to your government class on Election Day, after all the voting has occurred.

Some rules . . . because this *is*, admittedly, a simulation.

1. You CANNOT use social media (sorry, school rules), *but* you should describe how you WOULD use it in your campaign plan.
2. You should focus on *your* candidate and his or her merits. DO NOT play dirty politics. This is a simulation and not real life.
3. Your party platform cannot be "borrowed" from one of the major political parties of today. It needs to reflect your uniqueness and focus on the issues affecting Indiana voters.
4. Every group member needs to be an active participant in the party. Students who are absent need to continue to do their work digitally. Group members will assess collaboration for one another during the project.
5. Roles need to be assigned for each group member. Here are suggested ones:

    a. **Candidate**—Has to write, with help of other group members, and deliver a three- to five-minute speech on the day of the rally
    b. **Digital Media Consultant**—Primarily responsible for website and any other digital products that you will create
    c. **Print Media Consultant**—Oversees anything that is to be printed and/or displayed to promote your candidate and party
    d. **Campaign Manager**—Organizes the party platform and makes sure that everything aligns with that platform

Want to see additional examples of student overview sheets? Check out Appendix A for more!

It is also a best practice to ask students to engage with the project guidelines by having them reflect and restate the task ahead. Figures 10.5 and 10.6 provide sample activities for asking students to reflect on the early stages of the project launch and their role in the project ahead.

● **FIGURE 10.5** Sample Project Guidelines Process Check for Sixth Grade

Name: _____   Date: _____

Exit ticket directions:

Use this blank framework of the Golden Circle to put the purpose and actions of
our project in your own words.

I have shared an overview of my upcoming project with a parent or guardian.

x _____

(Parent Signature)

WHY

HOW

WHAT

● **FIGURE 10.6** Sample Project Guidelines Process Check for Ninth Grade

Portfolio Project Guidelines Exploration Activity

Instructions: Make a copy of this document and put it in your GFSF folder. Use this document to guide your
exploration of the project guidelines. After you explore the guidelines and fill in this document, create three
questions or "need to knows" about the project. These questions are what you feel you really "need to know." *Copy
and paste* this document into ECHO for submission. DO NOT LINK A GOOGLE DOC.

1. In one to two sentences, summarize what the rationale for this project is.
2. What is the driving question?
3. In one to two sentences, summarize the project overview.
4. What are the four phases of the portfolio? What do you need to do for each of these?
5. Explain what the Literacy Task is all about. When is the final draft due?
6. When is your final product due? What will your final product be? When are the final presentations?
7. What are two questions you have? (You may list more than two, but you need at least two).

**When I was in the classroom, the project launch was always an afterthought. I would
spend 10 to 20 hours planning a project that I thought would engage my students and
provide them with the opportunity to build valuable skills and master content, and
by the time that was done, I was exhausted! As I coach teachers now, the launch still
continues to be the last thing we chat about as they are running out the door to relieve
their sub from our project coaching hours. If you are feeling overwhelmed by designing
and facilitating your first project, then plan a hook that requires less preparation or
maybe just shoot for a couple of the elements of a project launch this time around; you
can go for all five components next time.**

The know/need to know process can be done in a variety of formats, including individual student reflection, small-group brainstorming, or whole-class discussion. Student responses can be recorded on poster paper or recorded digitally in a Google Doc, which proves to be especially helpful for teachers that have multiple classes working on the same project. See Figure 10.7 for two sample digital NTK charts for two block periods.

The Knows/Need to Knows

The need to know (NTK) process is the silver bullet for balancing student-guided and teacher-directed instruction in PBL. The NTK process (sometimes also referred to as "Know, Wonder, Learn") is a process that teachers can use to activate background knowledge on project topics and also use to generate student inquiry and ownership over learning.

On the first day of the project, the teacher outlines for students what they are going to be learning, doing, and creating. The teacher then asks the students, in a whole-class discussion, what they already know about or know how to do that relates to the project. The teacher charts or types student replies for documentation. The teacher then asks what students will need to learn about or learn how to do to be successful at the project deliverable. The teacher records student responses on chart paper or a Google Doc. From this list, the teacher uses what students come up with as "need to knows" (NTKs) to make daily connections to what students are learning about and, more importantly, why they are learning it.

● **FIGURE 10.7 Sample Digital Need to Know Charts**

Block 1

Knows	Need to Knows	Next Steps
• Presentations start on April 8th • Can do a puppet show, book • Creating a campaign against bullying • Targeted at either: elementary, middle, or high schoolers • Actual project is due one week before presentations • Has to do with WWII, Russian Revolution • Mini presentation on WWII • Reading *Animal Farm* • Analysis of fables • Going to write an essay on *Animal Farm* – will not be in class	• Do we have to present our answers to the questions on Drafting Your Story? • Will there be anything else we have to create for the final product? • Will we have work time in class next week? • Do we need to use a specific program to create the RSA? • Will the final presentation be formal? •	• Find out who will be on the panel • Look in the project briefcase for assignments created, extra resources • Come to class!! READ THE TEXTBOOK •

Block 2

Knows	Need to Knows	Next Steps
• Learning about bullies • Final product due March 29th • Make a Fable Style explanation of bullying • Make an anti-bullying campaign • Learning about Russian Revolution and WWII • Read *Animal Farm* • Groups • Mini presentation about WWII and Bullying • Fable Analysis • Tattoo Analysis • Write an essay • Create a story • Presentations begin April 8th • Final product due before Spring Break (present after Spring Break) • I have to create a puppet show, a storybook, or an RSA animate video • I have to choose 1-2 types of bullying • I have to bind the book (no staples please—consider a folder, binder, bound with twine, glue, etc.)	• How do you prevent bullying using non-violent methods? • How will I be graded? •	• Read textbook • Team Contract • Read *Animal Farm* • Start researching roles of countries in WWII • Learn what an RSA animate video is and how to make it • Research WWII and Russian Revolution • Research causes and effects of WWII • Identify how WWII connects to bullying • Identify themes in *Animal Farm* that relate to bullying • Talk to other teachers to find out which teachers will be involved • Review how to write a literary analysis essay? • Review past briefcases (resources) • Visit the How To Guides on Wednesday's agendas for making books, puppet shows, and RSAs

How-To: The Need to Know Process

Step 1: Anticipate what students will need to know based on content and skills of the project.

Step 2: Develop a launch that will activate need to knows.

Step 3: Collect and display knows and need to knows.

Step 4: Sort and map onto teaching and learning.

Step 5: Keep NTKs alive!

Tip: If the first time you attempt the K/ NTK process you find that your students are quiet, try having them write each idea (separate "knows" and "need to knows") on its own sticky note; then, ask them to come to the K/NTK poster and place their note near peers who have similar ideas. This will increase student participation!

The K/NTK process is critical to HQPBL. Check out the companion website (resources.corwin.com/ keepitrealPBLsecondary) for more on how to start your K/NTK chart, and be sure to keep it alive throughout the project as a means of student-driven learning!

What NTKs do you anticipate your students will come up with? Write them down here:

Are those reflected in activities you have planned already on your project calendar? Is there any wiggle room in your calendar in case a student takes you by surprise and wants to learn about something you weren't prepared for? If not, go back and give yourself a buffer or two in your project plans.

● **FIGURE 10.8** Step 1: Collect student ideas.

● **FIGURE 10.9** Step 2: Sort student need to knows by themes.

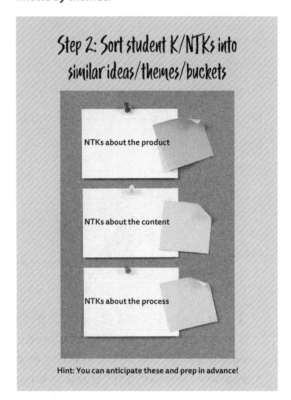

● **FIGURE 10.10** Step 3: Come back to your need to knows daily and make adjustments.

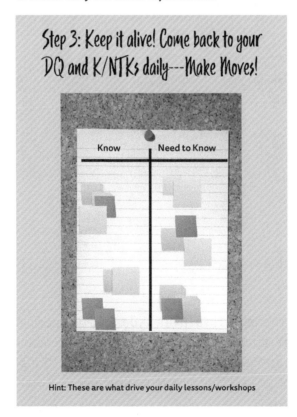

Project Groups

If the first benchmark for your project is collaborative, then at this time you can work on generating project groups and possibly even introduce students to their group members. This would be the time that you have groups engage in creating a group contract, which we discussed in the previous chapter.

Home Communication

On the day you launch your project, it is important to share the same information with your students' families. Communicating with parents and guardians allows everybody to be on the same page as it relates to what students are learning, how they are going to be learning it, how students will be assessed, and/or how the home can support your project. Here is a sample PBL letter; visit the companion website (resources.corwin.com/keepitrealPBLsecondary) to see another example:

Hello, Students, Parents, Guardians, & Friends of CCNTH!

It is with excitement that I write the second Entrepreneurial Mindsets/DireLights correspondence of the year! You are receiving this e-mail because you are connected with Central Coast New Tech High School in some way and/or you were recommended to me as an inspirational entrepreneur on the Central Coast. If you would prefer I take you off my e-mail list, please reply and let me know. If you have someone in mind that might be interested, please forward this e-mail to them and/or reply with their contact info.

Thank Yous!—Thank you to all of the volunteers who sat on our panel presentations for the Entrepreneurial Mindsets Gallery last month. Your feedback provided valuable next steps to all of our students for how to continue growing as professional communicators.

Projects!—DireLights ~ Let Some Light In!

We just rolled out our second project of the year, DireLights ~ Let Some Light In! To learn more about what we will be exploring this month, read the project guidelines. Students will be answering this driving question: What makes a business work? Students will be taking on the job responsibilities of the position they were hired for, as well as driving their own learning by choosing their own goals and tasks to keep the business running smoothly. They will be presenting their learning at various CCNTH event nights and field trips. To sign up to be a guest speaker, provide small-group interviews, and/or offer your feedback in any other way, please CLICK HERE to schedule a day and time to visit and work with us. To read about this authentic project and hear testimonials from last year's students, CLICK HERE.

(Continued)

(Continued)

Entrepreneurial Opportunities!

- Field trip to MoonRiver Salon & Spa Holiday MakerFaire/Market
  - On Friday, Dec 7, students will be setting up and selling DireLights candles alongside other craft artisans and professionals showcasing their products. Come support our students and do some holiday shopping!
  - Thank you, MoonRiver, for being stylists who support students!!

Next Steps!

- To keep up on what is happening in class and on campus, follow
  - @pbllab on Twitter
  - @direlights on Twitter, Instagram, Pinterest, and Facebook
  - @ccnth on Twitter, Instagram, and Facebook

- Please make note of important deadlines for the current project:
  - Blog Posts (Sundays at midnight)
  - Socratic Seminars (Mondays)
  - Benchmark 1 (due 11/15)
  - Benchmark 2 (due 12/4)
  - Benchmark 3 (due 12/11 or 12/13)
  - Benchmark 4 (due 3/18)
  - Benchmark 5 (due 3/19 or 3/21)
  - Final Products and Presentations (due 3/28)

Again, to sign up to be a guest speaker, provide small-group interviews, and/or offer your feedback in any other way, please CLICK HERE to schedule a day and time to visit and work with us.

Thank you,

Jennifer Stillittano

#realtalk: The more we communicate with parents, the less we need to communicate with parents. Preemptive PBL communication is critical!

Check out the companion website (resources.corwin.com/ keepitrealPBLsecondary) for more sample project newsletters to send home to parents and additional parent communication tips.

Chapter 11

Next Steps

Now that you have the foundational plans for your project, here are a few tips and resources to keep you moving in your planning.

Prototype Your Project

A best practice in PBL is for teachers to prototype the final product before they run the project. So roll up your sleeves and make whatever it is that you will be asking your students to make! This will give you an excellent idea of places that need further scaffolding and help you identify any hiccups before you run the project with your students.

Keep Building Those Reflection Skills

At the conclusion of every project, it is a best practice to require students to reflect on their learning. Unfortunately, because we teachers are always feeling behind due to the large time commitment that PBL requires, we often cut out the project reflection because we feel like we don't have enough time. You can ask students to reflect on the entire project process through any of the following:

- Digital vlog or blog sharing how they evolved with the project DQ
- Connections Protocol by National School Reform Faculty
- Journal using rubric language for thinking prompts

I encourage you to build in time into your project calendar for students to complete an in-depth reflection. Figure 11.1 shows a sample debrief from a 10th-grade humanities project, and you can also check out Appendix A for an example of a project reflection of the sixth-grade humanities project built throughout this book. You can also have students document and reflect on their growth through student-led conferences and/or the use of digital portfolios. See the companion website (resources.corwin.com/keepitrealPBLsecondary) for more information on this and an exemplar student digital portfolio.

● **FIGURE 11.1** "Back Off, You Big Bully" Project Debrief

At our school, the staff value clear student input. After each project, you will have the opportunity to share your thoughts and feelings about the work you just completed. This is a time for honest and critical feedback. For example, it is OK to say you did not like something, but be specific and explain what you did not like and why. The teachers will use your feedback in the evaluation of the past project as well as to prepare the next project.

1.   In your words, what was the goal or the objective of the project? Please be specific.
2.   What elements of the project did you enjoy? Why? Please be specific.
3.   What elements of the project need improvement? Why? How could they be improved? Please be specific.
4.   What specifically did you learn by doing the project?
5.   Think and reflect on the various teams (people) you have worked with since the beginning of the year. In which team did you feel the proudest of the final product you produced? Explain why.
6.   In which team did you feel the least proud of the final product you produced? Explain why.
7.   Did you research and answer *all* of the panel questions we gave you several weeks ago? If you received a score of 15 or above (75%) in the content literacy area, what specifically did you do to achieve this? If you received a score of 14 or below in the content literacy area, what do think you should have done differently?

Seek Out Collegial Feedback

Collegial feedback (see Figure 11.2) is another best practice that you can go about in multiple ways. Consider throwing your ideas for a project up on a poster. Next to it, put a grid on a second poster and label each of the quadrants one of the following: *Clarifying Questions*, *Probing Questions*, *Recommendations*, and *Resources*. This is a National School Reform Faculty (NSRF) protocol, and it's a great thing for you to leave hanging up in your faculty lounge. Teachers can look at it and think about pushing their practice as they think of questions or resources raised by your ideas. They may jot down a recommendation for a really great lesson they've seen. They might have a community connection for you that they can write under *Resources*. This is great way for you to live the PBL model yourself!

Photo courtesy of Chris Nelson Photography.

● **FIGURE 11.2** Jenny helping Lake Elementary teachers apply collegial feedback to their next project plans.

Plan for Exhibiting Student Work

Because your project plans are grounded in an authentic issue or problem in the community, there is a natural audience who could benefit from seeing your students' work. You will want to consider the logistics related to showcasing student work: Who should see the work? If it's a performance, where will you hold it and who will you invite? If it's a final product of some sort, where can the work temporarily "live"? And how do you want to present, or curate, the actual work so that it is aesthetically appealing and engaging to the audience? You may find the planning flow in Figure 11.3 useful, but presentation planning works better if it goes something like this:

You may even go so far as to enroll your colleagues in a Critical Friends protocol, which you can read more about on the companion website (resources.corwin.com/keepitrealPBLsecondary).

Prepare for the paradigm shift from open house to exhibition.

Plan for the end in mind—work backward from exhibition.

Design products that showcase HQPBL.

Schedule time to prepare for exhibition rehearsal and curation.

Curate beautiful work—drafting and feedback are required!

Honor the process of learning by displaying photos and drafts of student work throughout the entire project.

Prepare your audience—provide questions, sentence frames, or tasks for them to interact with students.

Debrief the exhibition experience with students the following day and celebrate!

Collect Community Connections

Community connections are so important for increasing the authenticity of your project plans. These connections can provide incredible learning experiences through real-world work, also referred to as "field work," within a project. See Figure 11.4 to help you get started with your field work plans.

Need some exhibition inspiration? Check out the companion website for videos and resources (resources.corwin.com/keepitrealPBLsecondary).

● **FIGURE 11.3** **Exhibition Checklist**

Exhibition Planning Flow
☐ Prepare for the paradigm shift.
☐ Plan for end in mind.
☐ Design products that showcase HQPBL.
☐ Schedule to prepare.
☐ Curate beautiful work.
☐ Honor the process of deeper learning.
☐ Prepare your audience.
☐ Debrief and celebrate it!

● **FIGURE 11.4** Planning Field Work Process Overview

Real World Exploration for Deeper Learning

A framework for planning meaningful learning experiences in the field

REAL WORLD EXPLORATION DEFINED:

A learning experience directly tied to current unit of study. Students should be dependent upon gaining information and skills during real world exploration to complete a larger piece of work. Information students gain from this experience cannot be retrieved from any other source-meaning it allows students to construct new, dynamic knowledge. - CraftED Curriculum

OVERVIEW

Define the purpose for real world exploration to enhance student learning

Define data collection methods

Work though logistics with experts or location

Prepare students for professional interactions with the field

Students interact with the field and document learning

Debrief learning and apply to final product/experience

For more teaching materials visit
www.craftedcurriculum.com

Real World Exploration Planning Flow

1. Start with a big idea, DQs for student learning in a unit.

2. Identify specific content, skills you want students to master.

3. Identify learning activities for the unit.

4. Identify where real world exploration can help students "go deeper."

5. Identify how/when students will apply what they learn from real world exploration.

YOU TRY!

1. ....

2. ....

3. ....

4. ....

5. ....

You can build a very simple database using a table in Google Docs to capture community connections. Start first by asking your parents to fill in a table like Table 11.1. Then, extend the request to your staff during the next staff meeting. Before you know it, you will have 50 community connections that you can pull from for guest speakers or field work locations for your project.

● TABLE 11.1 Community Connections Collection

Name/Contact Info	Current/Previous Employment	Professional Skills/Workforce Sector	Additional Talents	Community Memberships

Scaling and Sustaining HQPBL

Collaborate with your colleagues to review exemplary projects you find, possibly using any number of the lenses for Looking at Student Work (LASW) listed in Appendix C on the companion website at resources.corwin.com/keepitrealPBLsecondary. Consider what you like, notice what confuses you, and identify what may or may not work for your students. From there, your staff can calibrate on a shared vision for HQPBL (high-quality project-based learning). You can come back to this shared vision by reflecting and refining your project during a "project audit."

While it may be difficult to envision these next steps, know that there are always options available to you when you are ready to take your project to the next level. I strongly encourage you to pull your colleagues into your journey *now*—collaboration is an incredible support system as you venture into new instructional territory. A teacher from your same grade level could be a great planning partner; prior to running your project, a teacher from a grade above or below could give you valuable insight related to what skills students will need in the future or are lacking at the onset of the launch; and a new connection on Twitter could give you a great idea or resource to help save you time! We are all in this together. In the words of a fellow PBL colleague Drew Shrader, "It doesn't get easier—we just get better."

To learn more about engaging your staff in efforts to sustain HQPBL, check out a couple of articles provided in the companion website for step-by-step instructions (resources.corwin.com/keepitrealPBLsecondary).

"It doesn't get easier—we just get better." —Drew Schrader

Appendix Overview

Resource	Suggested Use/Reference
Resource A1.1 Sixth-Grade Humanities Project Overview: The Human Experience: Past to Present	Project plans presented as teacher moves and student outcomes. Referenced in every chapter of the book.
Resource A1.2 Sixth-Grade Project Assessment Tool: The Human Experience: Past to Present	Project rubric referenced in Chapter 7 to be used to evaluate student content and skill mastery.
Resource A1.3 Sixth-Grade Project Formative Assessment Map	Crosswalk exercise to ensure all benchmarks are formatively assessed using project rubric. Referenced in Chapter 7.
Resource A1.4 Sixth-Grade Project Calendar	"Big-picture" project calendar referenced in Chapter 8.
Resource A1.5 Sixth-Grade Humanities Project Launch Plans	Step-by-step teacher instructions for how to facilitate the model project launch. Referenced in Chapter 10.
Resource A1.6 Sixth-Grade Student Project Overview and Reflection	Student handout to provide an overview of the project and also to ask students to reflect on the work ahead. Referenced in Chapter 10.
Resource A1.7 Minilesson Outline: Photo Essay, Narrative Photography	Sample teacher daily lesson plans for project benchmarks.
Resource A2.1 Ninth-Grade Humanities Project Overview: "Reflections of a Hero" Project Guidelines	Sample project overview for ninth-grade humanities class.
Resource A2.2 Ninth-Grade Project Calendar	Sample ninth-grade project calendar.
Resource A2.3 Ninth-Grade Project Rubrics	Assessment tools for ninth-grade project.
Resource A2.4 Ninth-Grade Project Scaffold	Sample project scaffold for ninth-grade project.
Resource A2.5 Final Product Instructions	Student instructions for final product/presentation of the ninth-grade project.
Resource A2.6 Benchmark Assignment	Student instructions for benchmark assignment of artist statement.
Resource A3.1 12th-Grade Entrepreneurship Project Overview	Sample project overview for 12th-grade project.
Resource A3.2 12th-Grade Project Facilitation Notes	Teacher instructions for daily learning.
Resource A3.3 12th-Grade Project Calendar	Big-picture calendar for 12th-grade project.
Resource A3.4 12th-Grade Project Assessment Checklist	Grading checklist for student project work.
Resource A4.1 Assessment Tips and Tricks From the Trenches	Sample digital rubric reflection using Google Survey. Referenced in Chapter 7.
Resource A5.1 Sample Detailed Scope and Sequence for Ninth Grade	Sample scope and sequence for a year of PBL. Referenced in Chapter 4.

Resource C.1. General PBL Resources	These resources were referenced throughout the book and can be used for additional learning on the topic of PBL.
Resource C.2. Lenses for Looking At Student Work	These resources are helpful for coming up with definitions of high-quality PBL. Referenced in Chapter 1 and Chapter 11.
Resource C.3. Exemplar Projects	If you are looking for additional model projects, these resources will be helpful.
Resource C.4. Expert Rubrics	These are expert-designed PBL rubrics that teachers can use to build their rubrics. Referenced in Chapter 7.
Resource C.5. Student Learning Protocols	Protocols that are helpful for group work and classroom management. Referenced in Chapter 9.
Resource C.6. Project Launch Resources	Resources to support building project launches. Referenced in Chapter 10.
Resource C.7. Exhibiting Student Work	Resources to help teachers with "next steps" of PBL implementation, specific to Exhibition. Referenced in Chapter 11.
Resource C.8. Field Work	Resources to help teachers with "next steps" of PBL implementation, specific to integrating real-world connections and experts through field work. Referenced in Chapter 11.
Resource C.9. Parent Communication	Tips and resources to help teachers communicate with parents. Referenced in Chapter 10.
Resource C.10. PBL Professional Development	Resources for instructional leadership looking to implement and support PBL.

Appendix A

Complete Project Plans

● **RESOURCE A1.1** **Sixth-Grade Humanities Project Overview: The Human Experience: Past to Present**

Grade: 6   Content area: Humanities

Standards addressed:

Social Studies (CA) 6.1 Students describe what is known through archaeological studies of the early physical and cultural development of humankind from the Paleolithic era to the agricultural revolution.

6.1.1 Describe the hunter-gatherer societies, including the development of tools and the use of fire.

6.1.2 Identify the locations of human communities that populated the major regions of the world and describe how humans adapted to a variety of environments.

6.1.3 Discuss the climatic changes and human modifications of the physical environment that gave rise to the domestication of plants and animals and new sources of clothing and shelter.

*Possible SS connections:

6.4.2. Trace the transition from tyranny and oligarchy to early democratic forms of government and back to dictatorship in ancient Greece, including the significance of the invention of the idea of citizenship.

6.4.3. State the key differences between Athenian, or direct, democracy and representative democracy.

CCSS.ELA-LITERACY.W.6.1

Write arguments to support claims with clear reasons and relevant evidence.

CCSS.ELA-LITERACY.W.6.1.A

Introduce claim(s) and organize the reasons and evidence clearly.

CCSS.ELA-LITERACY.W.6.1.B

Support claim(s) with clear reasons and relevant evidence, using credible sources and demonstrating an understanding of the topic or text.

CCSS.ELA-LITERACY.W.6.1.C

Use words, phrases, and clauses to clarify the relationships among claim(s) and reasons.

CCSS.ELA-LITERACY.W.6.1.D

Establish and maintain a formal style.

CCSS.ELA-LITERACY.W.6.1.E

Provide a concluding statement or section that follows from the argument presented.

ELA (CCSS) CCSS.ELA-LITERACY.W.6.3

Write narratives to develop real or imagined experiences or events using effective technique, relevant descriptive details, and well-structured event sequences.

CCSS.ELA-LITERACY.W.6.3.A

Engage and orient the reader by establishing a context and introducing a narrator and/or characters; organize an event sequence that unfolds naturally and logically.

CCSS.ELA-LITERACY.W.6.3.B

Use narrative techniques, such as dialogue, pacing, and description, to develop experiences, events, and/or characters.

CCSS.ELA-LITERACY.W.6.3.C

Use a variety of transition words, phrases, and clauses to convey sequence and signal shifts from one time frame or setting to another.

CCSS.ELA-LITERACY.W.6.3.D

Use precise words and phrases, relevant descriptive details, and sensory language to convey experiences and events.

CCSS.ELA-LITERACY.W.6.3.E

Provide a conclusion that follows from the narrated experiences or events.

CCSS.ELA-LITERACY.W.6.5

With some guidance and support from peers and adults, develop and strengthen writing as needed by planning, revising, editing, rewriting, or trying a new approach. (Editing for conventions should demonstrate command of Language standards 1–3 up to and including Grade 6 here.)

CCSS.ELA-LITERACY.W.6.7

Conduct short research projects to answer a question, drawing on several sources and refocusing the inquiry when appropriate.

CCSS.ELA-LITERACY.W.6.8

Gather relevant information from multiple print and digital sources; assess the credibility of each source; and quote or paraphrase the data and conclusions of others while avoiding plagiarism and providing basic bibliographic information for sources.

CCSS.ELA-LITERACY.W.6.9

Draw evidence from literary or informational texts to support analysis, reflection, and research.

21st-century skills spotlight:

- Oral communication: Use of digital media/visual displays
- Collaboration: Commitment to shared success
- Agency: Impact self and community; use effort and practice to grow
- Written communication: Development, organization, language, and conventions

Project Design Framework

"The Human Experience: Past to Present"

Enduring Understanding: As humans, we adapt to our surroundings, and there are parallels between how early humans responded to life and the ways in which people in our community respond to life.

Driving Question: *What is the human experience of adapting to life? How are the current challenges of those living in San Francisco similar and different to those faced by early humans?*

Final Products: Photo essay, letter to local representative

Teacher Moves/Scaffolding	Student Actions/Outcomes
Project launch	**Students become familiar with project requirements and tasks.**
Benchmark #1: Early Humans	Deliverable: Early Humans Narrative
<ul><li>Come back to NTKs as driver for lessons during this benchmark phase.</li><li>Teacher will cover the topics as outlined in CA standards 6.1.1–3 through engaging activities of his or her choosing in addition to daily checks for understanding.</li><li>Teacher will assign students a scaffold assignment to help them consider the life of one early human during the time periods discussed in this benchmark. Teacher will collect and check for understanding of content.</li><li>Teacher will ask students to consider their Bio Sketch as they think about a firsthand account/narrative for this person may have sounded like. What feelings might they have had about his or her daily life?</li></ul>	<ul><li>Students will learn about early humans through engaging activities.</li><li>Students will consider the life of *one* early human and complete a Bio Sketch.</li><li>Students will learn about narrative writing techniques.</li><li>Students will write a first-person narrative on daily life, including tools used, migration, and environment.</li></ul>

(Continued)

Appendix A

Teacher Moves/Scaffolding	Student Actions/Outcomes
• Teacher will provide lessons on narrative writing techniques as outlined in CCSS to help students explain the feelings and experiences of early humans.	

Teacher Moves/Scaffolding	Student Actions/Outcomes
Benchmark #2: Compare/Contrast Past to Present	**Deliverable:** 2 Voice Poetry
• Come back to NTKs as driver for lessons during this benchmark phase. • Teacher will collect local news stories through a variety of mediums. Teacher will then facilitate a jigsaw lesson for students to learn about local issues in the community. Lesson will conclude with a class discussion or Socratic Seminar on key themes/issues in the community. • Teacher will prepare students to go on a walking field trip to address the DQs: *What social issues are present in our local community? What do we see? What can we infer?* • Teacher will debrief field work experience. • Teacher will ask students to consider this: *"How is what we have learned about local community issues similar and different from issues that early humans faced in our previous studies?"* Teacher will then assign a Venn diagram graphic organizer for students to complete. • After Venn diagram approval, teacher will then provide a writing workshop on 2 voice poetry. Teacher will bring students back to the project DQ as the driver for this benchmark deliverable. See instructions provided separately.	• Students will revisit project overview and reconsider what they now know and what they need to know in order to complete Benchmark #2. • Students will learn and discuss local community issues. • Students will engage in field work to make observations about local community issues. Students will take photos to highlight this experience (to be used later for photo essays). • Students will process and analyze their field work experience. • Students will compare and contrast local issues with early humans and will turn in a Venn diagram to show understanding of these. • Students will write and record 2 voice poetry to show their understanding of the similarities and differences of the human experience.
Benchmark #3: Community Issues	**Deliverable:** Infographic
• Come back to NTKs as driver for lessons during this benchmark phase. • Teacher will assign students to begin group research on identified topic (community issue) of choice. • Teacher may decide to use the field work as a focus for the Question Formulation Technique for students to develop group driving questions for future research on local issues. • Teacher should be sure to review source credibility, bias, and proper citations. • Teacher may decide to bring in experts to discuss local issues as a form of field work. • Teacher will provide a workshop on how to create an infographic as a way to distill group research into the most engaging and simplest format. • Possible math and NGSS connections can be made by teacher.	• Students will work with a small group to conduct research on a topic of choice related to a local community issue and turn in research documentation, as assigned by teacher. • Students *may* interview an expert on a topic of local issue. • Students will work with a small group to create an infographic to display research knowledge on a local community issue.

Teacher Moves/Scaffolding	Student Actions/Outcomes
<u>Benchmark #4</u>: Human Stories/Experiences Related to Community Issues • Prior to the beginning of this benchmark phase, the teacher will want to identify a location for curating completed student photo essays. • Come back to NTKs as driver for lessons during this benchmark phase. • Teacher will introduce students to the concept of photo essays and analyze models using an Artful Thinking Routine. • Teacher will provide a tech tutorial on how to edit photographs taken during previous field work. • Teacher will provide a workshop on how to create a photo essay. • Teacher may decide to have students complete a writing assignment to accompany photographs that includes narratives, subtitles, or informational writing. • Teacher will ask students to come back to the project DQ as the prompt for developing a photo essay.	<u>Deliverable</u>: Photo Essay • Students will review exemplary models of photo essays to develop a "north star" for their work. • Students will learn how to create a photo essay that addresses the project DQ. • Students will digitally edit photographs from field work. • Students *may* complete a writing assignment to accompany photo essays. • Students will curate photo essays in the community.
<u>Benchmark #5</u>: Civic Engagement • Come back to NTKs as driver for lessons during this benchmark phase. • Teacher may choose to cover citizenship and democracy in Greece through engaging history lessons. • Teacher will discuss the power of our voice and our role as citizens in a democracy. Teacher will help students identify an appropriate government representative or organization recipient for a letter they will be writing to persuade them to take action on a local community issue they have studied. • Teacher will facilitate a writing workshop on how to write formal letters with a strong claim and reasoning. • Teacher will take students through the entire writing process.	<u>Deliverable</u>: Letter to Representative • Students *may* learn about early democracy and citizenship in Greece. • Students will learn how to develop a claim with logical reasoning. • Students will write a letter to a local representative to advocate for a change/improvement to a local issue. • Students will participate in the entire writing (revision) process. • Students will mail their letters.

Project Reflection
 	
 • Teacher will ask students to reflect on the entire project process through any of the following:
    o Digital vlog or blog sharing how they evolved with the project DQ
    o Connections Protocol
    o Journal using rubric language for thinking prompts
	Deliverable: Reflection
	
	 • Students will reflect on their learning throughout the process of this project.

Appendix A

• **RESOURCE A1.2** Sixth-Grade Project Assessment Tool: The Human Experience: Past to Present

	Emerging	Developing	Proficient High School Ready	Advanced High School Level
Oral Communication: Use of digital media/visual displays *What is the evidence that the student can use digital media/visual displays to engage and support audience understanding?*	Digital media or visual displays are confusing, extraneous, or distracting.	Digital media or visual displays are primarily informative and relevant, but some elements are confusing, extraneous, or distracting.	Digital media or visual displays are informative and relevant.	Digital media or visual displays are appealing, informative, and support audience engagement and understanding.
Collaboration: Commitment to shared success	• Cannot describe what constitutes success for the team's task. • Impedes team progress by failing to complete individual tasks on time. • Provides unhelpful negative feedback.	• Generally describes what constitutes success in the context of the team's task. • Mostly completes individual tasks on time but needs reminding.	• Clearly and specifically describes what constitutes success in the context of the team's task. • Completes individual tasks on time and with sufficient quality. • Provides positive and constructive feedback to team members. • Devotes time and effort to ensure team benchmarks and due dates are met.	In addition, . . . • Supports others to complete necessary work and ensure the team's success. • Actively encourages and motivates others to attain high levels of achievement.
Agency: Impact self and community	Identifies the current status of the classroom and home community but not the ups and downs over time.	Has limited understanding of individual role in the ups and downs of the classroom and home community.	Identifies individual role in the ups and downs of the classroom and home community.	Analyzes individual role in the ups and downs of the classroom and home community.
Agency: Use effort and practice to grow	Does not connect effort or practice to getting better at a skill.	Superficially connects effort and practice to getting better at skills.	Understands how effort and practice relate to getting better at skills and improved work quality.	Understands how effort and practice relate to getting better at skills, improved work quality, or performance.

	Emerging	Developing	Proficient — High School Ready	Advanced — High School Level
Written Communication: Development — *What is the evidence that the student can develop ideas?*	• Does not explain background or context of topic/issue. • Controlling idea* is unclear or not evident throughout the writing. • Ideas and evidence are underdeveloped.	• Provides a simplistic or partial explanation of background and context of topic/issue. • Controlling idea* is present but unevenly addressed throughout the writing. • Ideas and evidence are somewhat developed.	• Provides a partial explanation of background and context of topic/issue. • Controlling idea is evident but may not be present throughout the text. • Ideas and evidence are mostly developed.	• Addresses appropriate background and context of topic/issue. • Controlling idea* is presented clearly throughout the writing. • Ideas and evidence are developed.
Written Communication: Organization — *What is the evidence that the student can organize and structure ideas for effective communication?*	• Ideas and evidence are disorganized, making relationships unclear. • No transitions are used, or are used ineffectively. • Conclusion, when appropriate, is absent or restates the introduction or prompt.	• Ideas and evidence are loosely sequenced or organized; there is some sense of relationships. • Transitions connect ideas with some lapses; may be repetitive or formulaic. • Conclusion, when appropriate, follows from the controlling idea.	• Ideas and evidence are organized to show relationships, though organization may be formulaic. • Transitions connect ideas. • Conclusion, when appropriate, follows from and supports the controlling idea.	• Ideas and evidence are sequenced to show relationships. • Transitions are varied and connect ideas, showing clear relationships. • Conclusion, when appropriate, is logical and raises important implications.
Written Communication: Language and conventions — *What is the evidence that the student can use language skillfully to communicate ideas?*	• Language, style, and tone are inappropriate to the purpose, task, and audience. • Uses norms and conventions of writing that are inappropriate to the discipline/genre.** • Has an accumulation of errors in grammar, usage, and mechanics that distract or interfere with meaning.	• Language, style, and tone are somewhat appropriate to the purpose, task, and audience. • Uses norms and conventions of writing that are mostly inappropriate to the discipline/genre.** • Has some minor errors in grammar, usage, and mechanics that partially distract or interfere with meaning.	• Language and tone are mostly appropriate to the purpose, task, and audience. • Attempts to follow the norms and conventions of writing in the discipline/genre.** • Is generally free of distracting errors in grammar, usage, and mechanics.	• Language, style, and tone are appropriate to the purpose, task, and audience. • Follows the norms and conventions of writing in the discipline/genre** with some errors. • Is free of distracting errors in grammar, usage, and mechanics.

(Continued)

	Emerging	Developing	Proficient High School Ready	Advanced High School Level
	• Textual citation, when appropriate, is missing or incorrect.	• Cites textual evidence, partially or using an incorrect format, when appropriate.	• Cites textual evidence with some errors, when appropriate.	• Cites textual evidence with some minor errors, when appropriate.
Social Studies: **Early Humans, Human Behavior**	Student is developing in ability to describe and connect early physical and cultural developments across time periods. Student may have limited recall of content vocabulary, events, and locations. Student may not be able to discuss impacts of key events.	6.1 Student can describe what is known through archaeological studies of the early physical and cultural development of humankind from the Paleolithic era to the agricultural revolution. • Describe the hunter-gatherer societies, including the development of tools and the use of fire. • Identify the locations of human communities that populated the major regions of the world and describe how humans adapted to a variety of environments. • Discuss the climatic changes and human modifications of the physical environment that gave rise to the domestication of plants and animals and new sources of clothing and shelter.	In addition, . . . • Makes connections to modern-day local community issues.	In addition, . . . • Makes connections to modern global issues. • Uses supposition to predict the potential future impact.

Social Studies: Citizenship	Emerging	Developing	Proficient High School Ready	Advanced High School Level
	Student is developing in ability to analyze the geographic, political, economic, religious, and social structures of early civilizations of Ancient Greece. Student may struggle to make connections or comparisons.	6.4 Student can analyze the geographic, political, economic, religious, and social structures of the early civilizations of Ancient Greece. • Trace the transition from tyranny and oligarchy to early democratic forms of government and back to dictatorship in ancient Greece, including the significance of the invention of the idea of citizenship (e.g., from Pericles' Funeral Oration). • State the key differences between Athenian, or direct, democracy and representative democracy.	In addition,.... • Makes the connection to modern-day citizenship and participation.	In addition,.... • Articulates one's individual role in a democracy.

(Continued)

Appendix A

• **RESOURCE A1.2** (Continued)

	Emerging	Developing	Proficient High School Ready	Advanced High School Level
ELA Research: Research to build and present knowledge	• Student is not yet able to conduct research projects independently. • Student is able to gather information from a single source, but may struggle to assess its credibility and/or effectively paraphrase the content. • Student is developing in ability to draw upon data to support his or her reflection, analysis, or research.	• CCSS.ELA-LITERACY.W.6.7 Conduct short research projects to answer a question, drawing on several sources and refocusing the inquiry when appropriate. • CCSS.ELA-LITERACY.W.6.8 Gather relevant information from multiple print and digital sources; assess the credibility of each source; and quote or paraphrase the data and conclusions of others while avoiding plagiarism and providing basic bibliographic information for sources. • CCSS.ELA-LITERACY.W.6.9 Draw evidence from literary or informational texts to support analysis, reflection, and research.	In addition,… • Makes further inquiry through additional research questions. • Gathers information from guest speakers and show proper citations when paraphrasing. • Draws evidence from a wide variety of sources to support analysis, reflection, and research.	In addition,… • Engages in lengthier research projects driven by complexity of inquiry and interest. • Gathers information from nontraditional sources through independent field work interactions. • Properly paraphrases, documents, and cites such interactions. • Draws evidence from a variety of sources, including field work, to support analysis, reflection, and research.

*Controlling idea may refer to a thesis, argument, topic, or main idea, depending on the type of writing.

Original rubrics created by New Tech Network with support from Stanford Center for Assessment, Learning, and Equity (SCALE) and based on similar rubrics from Envision Schools. @Copyright New Tech Network 2016. Modifications to rubric made by CraftED Curriculum, LLC in support of project design for Innovate Public Schools.

• **RESOURCE A1.3** Sixth-Grade Project Formative Assessment Map

Benchmark: Deliverable	Rubric Rows for Formative Assessment
#1 Early Humans: Narrative	Written Communication: Language and conventions SS: Early Humans, Human Behavior
#2 Compare/Contrast: 2 Voice Poetry	Written Communication: Organization and collaboration Oral Communication: Use of digital media/visual displays SS: Early Humans, Human Behavior
#3 Community Issues: Infographic	Collaboration ELA research
#4 Human Stories: Photo essay	Collaboration Agency: Impact self and community Agency: Use effort to practice and grow Oral Communication: Use of digital media/visual displays Written communication: Language and conventions
#5 Civic Engagement: Letter to representative	Written Communication: Development Written Communication: Language and conventions Agency: Impact self and community Agency: Use effort to practice and grow

● RESOURCE A1.4 Sixth-Grade Project Calendar

	Monday	Tuesday	Wednesday	Thursday	Friday
Week 1 **Benchmark #1**	Project launch!	Early humans	Early humans	Early humans	Complete case study profile
Week 2 **Benchmark #1**	WW: Narrative writing, brainstorm	Complete narrative writing draft #1	Revise narrative writing (self, peer)	Draft #2 of narrative writing	**Benchmark #1 due:** **Complete narrative writing**
Week 3 **Benchmark #2**	Intro to local issues	Walking field trip	Identify group topics for research via QFT process	Group research	Group research
Week 4 **Benchmark #2**	Prep for field work interviews	Turn in interview questions, role-play	Conduct field work interviews	Debrief interviews	**Benchmark #2 due:** **Venn diagram**
Week 5 **Benchmark #3**	WW: Intro to 2 voice poetry	Revise writing	Audio record	Edits	**Benchmark #3 due:** **Final 2 voice poetry due**
Week 6 **Benchmark #4**	Additional group research	Experts visit, field work	WW: Citations	Intro to infographics	Group work on infographics
week 7 **Benchmark #4**	Group work on infographics	**Benchmark #4 due:** **Groups turn in infographics**	Intro to photo editing	Digital edits	WW: Photo essays
Week 8 **Benchmark #5**	Draft #1 of photo essays	Revisions, feedback (self, peer)	Draft #2 of photo essays	**Benchmark #5 due:** **Photo essays**	
Week 9 **Benchmark #6/ final**	Lesson: Our voice, identifying recipient	WW: Formal letter (claim, persuasive language, effective comm.)	Draft #1 of letter	Revisions, feedback (self, peer)	**Final due: Draft #2 of letter**
Week 10	Exhibition prep and final project reflections—>			Exhibition	

*WW: Writers Workshop

● **RESOURCE A1.5** **Sixth-Grade Humanities Project Launch Plans**

Phase	Teacher Moves	Student Actions, Outcomes
1: Simulation	The teacher explains that today we are going to be engaging in a simulation, and although it may feel as if we are talking about a *long* time ago, maybe we will begin to see some connections to us today.	Students participate in simulation to excite them about the content of this project.
2: Debrief	Teacher will pose the following questions to the class for a whole-group discussion: – What did you notice about your behavior? Others' behavior? – What surprised you? – What does this remind you of? – How is it same/different from the ways in which we behave/respond today? *Teacher may choose to do this as a "Think/Pair/Share" or an in-depth Socratic Seminar.	Students will verbally make the connections between ancient humans behaviors and current human behaviors/adaptations to living in their surroundings.
3: Intro to project	Teacher will pass out student project overview sheets. Teacher says, "Let's look at a few models of the kind of work you will be engaging in during this project." Teacher will show chosen models of final products (photo essays, 2 voice poetry, letters to government representatives) and ask students to journal and then discuss the visible thinking routine "See, Think, Wonder."	Students will review project sheet using popcorn reading strategy in small groups. Students will analyze exemplar models to inform their "north star" for this project and help initiate questions for N/NTK process next.
4: K/NTKs	Teacher will provide students with five sticky notes and ask them to write down what they know about the project and what they think they need to know. Then, place sticky notes on appropriate place on class T-chart. Teacher should remind students to write their names on the sticky notes. After students have completed this exercise, teacher should categorize and prioritize students NTKs for future workshops.	Students will be able to articulate what they know about this project (content and skills) and what they need to know, in order to drive their learning by engaging in the K/NTK process.
Exit ticket	Teacher shows the Simon Sinek *Golden Circle* TED Talk video to students then asks them to complete Golden Circle diagram on project sheet.	Students complete the exit ticket for teacher approval, but keep the form for their reference and parent signature.

● **RESOURCE A1.6** Sixth-Grade Student Project Overview and Reflection

"The Human Experience: Past to Present"

Student Project Overview

Driving Question: *What is the human experience of adapting to life? How are the current challenges of those living in San Francisco similar and different to those faced by early humans?*

Why: As humans, we tend to naturally categorize and isolate ourselves by finding the many ways in which we are different; however, history, specifically early humans, will show us that we are more alike than we are different—how we adapt, how we migrate, and how we fill our needs. History can also help us better understand, appreciate, and improve the world around us with laws, behaviors, systems, and structures. With this knowledge, we become empowered and possess the ability to be advocates for change in our community.

How: We are going to learn a lot during this project—from the Paleolithic era to the agricultural revolution, to writing, to effectively speaking, to creative uses of technology, to curating our work, and to advocating for our community. We will engage in field work, speak to community members, participate in writing workshops and class discussions, work with our peers, and think deeply and passionately. We will provide each other feedback to develop our very best work that will be shared with a public audience.

What: We will be using technology to research, make infographics, record 2 voice poetry, and document human experiences through photography. We will learn how to write a professional letter to a government official and how to tell a human story through narrative writing and photo essays.

Name: _____   Date: _____

Exit ticket directions:

Use this blank framework of the Golden Circle to put the purpose and actions of our project in your own words.

I have shared an overview of my upcoming project with a parent or guardian.

x _____

(Parent Signature)

● **RESOURCE A1.7** Minilesson Outline: Photo Essay, Narrative Photography

1. What are photo essays/narrative photography?
    1. Background
        1. The Narrative Photography Competition in Portland, Oregon, describes the concept in the following way: "The power of narrative, or storytelling, is at the foundation of much of photography. Photographers are creating complex and descriptive moments in time. Contemporary photographers are crafting and documenting new forms of a visual short story."
    2. How is narrative photography similar to the basic structure of a story?
2. Models
    1. View models and have students journal using visible thinking routine.
        1. "Too Tired for Sunshine"
        2. "Day in the Life of a Model"
        3. "Daily Life of Detroit"

3. Traits of effective narrative photography/photo essays

    1. Have class discuss what they journaled and chart on board.

    2. Ask students, based on the above, what do we think makes for an effective photo essay/narrative photography.

4. Writing techniques

    1. Depending on your content, you may wish to visit literary devices or narrative techniques to enhance student drafts.

5. Publishing, curating final products

    1. Publish any related writing and photographs.

    2. Frame and hang in public location, possibly a library or museum.

Activity:

2 Voice Poetry

Instructions:

Compare and contrast the experience of two individuals. Using a basic Venn diagram, share how the emotions and experiences of these two unique individuals may have obvious differences but also common human threads.

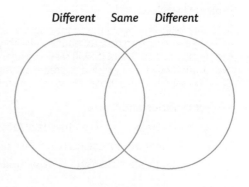

Your Venn diagram will help you to complete a piece of 2 voice poetry, which is an effective form of writing to show similarities and differences or harmony and discord. It allows for a dynamic blend of monologue by and dialogue between two unique perspectives/voices. A 2 voice poem is written in two columns. Two students read the poem, and each chooses a column to read. When there are words that appear on the same line, the students read those words in unison. Read the example provided (Graphic 1) and use the worksheet (Graphic 2) to help you write your poem. Be sure to include narrative writing techniques such as dialogue and sensory language to enhance your poetry.

Work through the entire writing process to ensure your best quality of work. Then, proceed to record your poetry, with the help of an additional voice, through a recording program.

Voice 1: _____ (Unique/Different perspective)	Both Voices (What human traits are shared/in common?)	Voice 2: _____ (Unique/Different perspective)

• RESOURCE A2.1 Ninth-Grade Humanities Project Overview:
"Reflections of a Hero" Project Guidelines

Rationale:

The Odyssey is a Greek classic in the form of an epic poem that tells the story of an individual trying to get home while overcoming multiple challenges along the way. It uses the structures of the Hero's Journey, asks questions about the moral compass of a person, and focuses on "classic" themes. The epic poem provides a unique model to reflect upon each student's journey this past year at CCNTH. When thinking about your journey, what struggles and challenges have you overcome? How are you a hero?

Driving Question:

1. What can an exploration of a classic hero tell a modern audience about the nature of a "hero" today?

Subquestion:

1. What are the key elements of a Hero's Journey?
2. How are *you* a hero?

Project Overview:

Students will begin by exploring the question of what makes a hero. They will then watch *Forrest Gump in a Minute* to gain perspective on how to reduce a big story to a relatively short time period while incorporating elements of the Hero's Journey. Students will read and analyze excerpts of *The Odyssey* and review how to think about their own lives as historians. Their task is to create a 1-minute reflection of their personal "Hero's Journey" while at Central Coast New Tech High School.. Open this link for a complete description of the Hero's Journey Final Product.

Project Duration and Teams:

*   This project begins on Tuesday, May 22, 2020, and ends on Thursday, June 6, 2020.
*   Student will choose his or her own teams.
    *   Students can choose to work alone, with one other person, or in a group of no more than three.

Major Benchmarks:

*   Analysis of selections from *The Odyssey*
*   Drafting your journey
*   Comparison to *The Odyssey* journal

Major Due Dates (in list form):

Project Calendar

Read selections from *The Odyssey*—5/21 and 5/22

3. Table discussion questions from *The Odyssey*—5/23
4. Drafting your journey—5/28
5. Create rubric—5/29
6. Final product of your Hero's Journey—6/3
7. Artist's statement about your Hero's Journey—6/4
1. Audience responses to your Hero's Journey—6/4
2. Student assessment (using the rubric you created) of your Hero's Journey Final Product—6/5
3. Student reflection—6/5
4. Comparison to *The Odyssey* in-class essay—6/5
5. Share-out of one challenge and connections to *The Odyssey*—6/6

California State Content Standards

English:

3.0 Literary Response and Analysis

3.1 Articulate the relationship between the expressed purposes and the characteristics of different forms of dramatic literature (e.g., comedy, tragedy, drama, dramatic monologue).

3.2 Compare and contrast the presentation of a similar theme or topic across genres to explain how the selection of genre shapes the theme or topic.

3.5 Compare works that express a universal theme and provide evidence to support the ideas expressed in each work.

2.1 Write biographical or autobiographical narratives or short stories:

  a. Relate a sequence of events and communicate the significance of the events to the audience.

  b. Locate scenes and incidents in specific places.

  c. Describe with concrete sensory details the sights, sounds, and smells of a scene and the specific actions, movements, gestures, and feelings of the characters; use interior monologue to depict the characters' feelings.

  d. Pace the presentation of actions to accommodate changes in time and mood.

  e. Make effective use of descriptions of appearance, images, shifting perspectives, and sensory details.

2.2 Write responses to literature:

  a. Demonstrate a comprehensive grasp of the significant ideas of literary works.

  b. Support important ideas and viewpoints through accurate and detailed references to the text or to other works.

1.0 Listening and Speaking Strategies

1.1 Formulate judgments about the ideas under discussion and support those judgments with convincing evidence.

1.7 Use props, visual aids, graphs, and electronic media to enhance the appeal and accuracy of presentations.

2.4 Deliver oral responses to literature:

  a. Advance a judgment demonstrating a comprehensive grasp of the significant ideas of works or passages (i.e., make and support warranted assertions about the text).

  b. Support important ideas and viewpoints through accurate and detailed references to the text or to other works.

History:

Chronological and Spatial Thinking

  1. Students compare the present with the past, evaluating the consequences of past events and decisions and determining the lessons that were learned.

  2. Students analyze how change happens at different rates at different times; understand that some aspects can change while others remain the same; and understand that change is complicated and affects not only technology and politics but also values and beliefs.

  3. Students use a variety of maps and documents to interpret human movement, including major patterns of domestic and international migration, changing environmental preferences and settlement patterns, the frictions that develop between population groups, and the diffusion of ideas, technological innovations, and goods.

  4. Students relate current events to the physical and human characteristics of places and regions.

Common Core SS Literacy Standards:

CCSS.ELA-Literacy.RH.9-10.3 Analyze in detail a series of events described in a text; determine whether earlier events caused later ones or simply preceded them.

CCSS.ELA-Literacy.RH.9-10.8 Assess the extent to which the reasoning and evidence in a text support the author's claims.

Common Core CCR Standards:

CCSS.ELA-Literacy.CCRA.SL.4 Present information, findings, and supporting evidence such that listeners can follow the line of reasoning and the organization, development, and style are appropriate to task, purpose, and audience.

CCSS.ELA-Literacy.CCRA.SL.5 Make strategic use of digital media and visual displays of data to express information and enhance understanding of presentations.

CCSS.ELA-Literacy.CCRA.SL.6 Adapt speech to a variety of contexts and communicative tasks, demonstrating command of formal English when indicated or appropriate.

CCSS.ELA-Literacy.CCRA.W.3 Write narratives to develop real or imagined experiences or events using effective technique, well-chosen details, and well-structured event sequences.

● **RESOURCE A2.2** Ninth-Grade Project Calendar

Monday	Tuesday	Wednesday	Thursday	Friday
20 *Isbell/Holst gone from 11–3* Art of Argument Ends	21 Reflections of a Hero Entry Event— 5. What Is a Hero Journal? 6. Prezi or TED (What Is a Hero start @~19:00) 7. Hero's Journey 8. CCNTH in a minute (Love to write and produce this with staff; see Hero's Journey video for a guide) 9. If you were to reduce your year at CCNTH into 1 minute, what would it look like? 10. Project Guidelines 11. *Odyssey* Video and Hero's Journey PPT Students read their sections in class & for HW	22 K/NTK/NS Read *Odyssey*	23 *Holst and Isbell Gone at Common Core SLOCOE* Holden leads Discuss/Analyze *Odyssey* and Hero's Journey	24 Rally Schedule Isbell- How do you think like a Historian? Identify Group (1, 2, 3 people) Identify Audience Identify Challenges (at least 4) Identify Medium (Movie in a Minute, Song, Photo Essay, Painting/Art, 1-minute speech, etc.) Begin draft (due 5/28) No School
27 No School	28 Draft of Journey due – *Holst out with incoming 9th-grade day* – *Isbell out in VFW presentations*	29 – *Holst out with incoming 9th-grade day* – *Isbell out in VFW presentations* Create rubric (due by the end of class)	30 (early out) Work Time	31 Work Time

Monday	Tuesday	Wednesday	Thursday	Friday
3 Work Time	4 Work Time Final Product due today Audience Reflections due today	5 Artist Statement due today Student Assessment, Reflection, & Connections to *Odyssey* completed in class today	6 Small-Group Share Out (1 challenge) Viewing Questions due no later than today	7 Last Day of School

● **RESOURCE A2.3** **Ninth-Grade Project Rubrics**

CRITERIA	Scoring Element	UNSATISFACTORY (Below Performance Standards)	PROFICIENT (Minimal Criteria)	ADVANCED (Demonstrates Exceptional Performance)
Critical Thinking Explanation of Challenge Connections to *The Odyssey* Connections to Hero's Journey	**CT**	• Vague or lacking a clear description of the challenge • Vague or unclear explanation as to how the challenge was overcome • Vague or unclear analysis as to how the challenge is similar to a challenge found in *The Odyssey* • Vague or unclear analysis as to where the challenge fits into the Hero's Journey	Adequate description of the challenge General explanation as to how the challenge was overcome Explanation as to how the challenge is similar to a challenge found in *The Odyssey* is supported with at least one concrete detail Analysis as to where the challenge fits into the Hero's Journey is supported with at least one concrete detail	In addition to meeting the PROFICIENT criteria... • Description of student's challenge is significant and complex • Complex explanation as to how the challenge was overcome • Explanation as to how the challenge is similar to a challenge found in *The Odyssey* is supported with at least three concrete details • Analysis as to where the challenge fits into the Hero's Journey is supported with at least three concrete details
		8 - - - - - 13	14 - - - - 17	18 - - - - - 20

(Continued)

● **RESOURCE A2.3** (Continued)

CRITERIA	Scoring Element	UNSATISFACTORY (Below Performance Standards)	PROFICIENT (Minimal Criteria)	ADVANCED (Demonstrates Exceptional Performance)
Vocal Expression Physical Characteristics Appropriateness of Content and Language **(Individual)**	**EC**	• Speaker hard to hear or understand • Voice or tone distracted from purpose of presentation • Excessive use of verbal fillers • Little eye contact with audience • Movements stiff or unnatural • Inappropriate language, content, or examples for this audience	• Speaker easy to hear and understand • Tone conversational but with purpose and matches intent • Voice sounded natural, neither patterned nor monotone • Words pronounced clearly, correctly, and without verbal fillers • Strong eye contact with entire audience • Gestures and movements natural and effective • Speaker obviously considered the audience; used appropriate language and examples	In addition to meeting the *Proficient* criteria . . . • Speaker enjoyable to hear; used expression and emphasis • Speaker used voice to create emotional response in audience • Examples and words creative and well-chosen for target audience • Overall presentation creative and exciting
		8 - - - - - - - - - - - - - - - - -13	14 - - - - - - - - - - - - - - - 17	18 - - - - - - - - - - - - - -20

● **RESOURCE A2.4** Ninth-Grade Project Scaffold

Drafting Your Journey

Objective: Please answer each of the following questions using complete sentences. If you are working with other people, please list all names and use different colors. *If you are working with other people, all members must answer each question.*

1. Who will you work with (you can work by yourself, with one person, or with two people)?

2. Who is your audience for your Hero's Journey?

3. Why did you choose this audience?

4. What are three challenges you have faced this year?

5. Why did you choose each of the challenges?

6. How did you overcome each challenge?

7. In what ways are *you* a hero?

8. What type of medium will you use? Choices include Movie in a Minute, song (lyrics and music), photo essay, painting/drawing, RSA Animate, Xtranormal or GoAnimate, 1-minute speech, and so on.

9. Why did you choose this medium?

10. Now, please complete this storyboard:

Break your story into the three different challenges you have faced.

Next, write down the important facts for each of your challenges; make sure you focus on describing the challenge, its impact on you, why it is significant, how you overcame it, and how you are a hero.

Describe, create, or find the image(s) you will be using to illustrate this point.

#1 Image: Significant Point:	#2 Image: Significant Point:	#3 Image: Significant Point:
1. What is the challenge?	1. What is the challenge?	1. What is the challenge?
2. What is the impact of this specific challenge?	2. What is the impact of this specific challenge?	2. What is the impact of this specific challenge?
3. Why is this a significant challenge?	3. Why is this a significant challenge?	3. Why is this a significant challenge?
4. How did you overcome this challenge?	4. How did you overcome this challenge?	4. How did you overcome this challenge?
5. How/Why are you a hero?	5. How/Why are you a hero?	5. How/Why are you a hero?

● RESOURCE A2.5 Final Product Instructions

Now it is time to submit this and begin your final product.

Objective:

● Please create a 1-minute presentation that identifies a minimum of three challenges you have faced and overcome this year at Central Coast New Tech High School (challenges do not necessarily have to come from school). How are you a hero? The focus is to reflect on how you have grown as a person this year. Remember to think like a historian.

Due Date:

● Your Hero's Journey Final Product is due no later than Tuesday, June 4.

Audience and Presentation:

● Please identify an audience for your presentation. Please note that your presentation for this project will be different than presentations in the past. You will not present your Hero's Journey to the class. You will choose the audience and present your Hero's Journey product to that audience.

  ○ Audience can include any of the following:

    ■ Parents, friends, family members, other adults in your life (coach, youth pastor, Boy Scout Leader, etc.), yourself

  ○ Your audience will provide you with feedback based on your presentation (questions to be provided by you and your teachers).

(Continued)

● **RESOURCE A2.5** (Continued)

Grading:

- Your Hero's Journey will be graded using a rubric by yourself and one of your World Studies teachers.
- You will create the rubric for your Hero's Journey.

Details:

1. Hero's Journey Presentations are limited to one minute (only).

2. You choose the medium: 1-minute video (similar to *Forrest Gump in a Minute*), RSA Animate, XtraNormal or GoAnimate, painting or drawing, original song (lyrics and music), photo essay, something else (you choose and tell one of the World Studies teachers).

3. Your Hero's Journey must identify and explain at least ***three*** challenges you have faced this year.

4. Your Hero's Journey must identify and explain how you overcame each of your challenges.

5. Your Hero's Journey should analyze and explain how you are a hero.

6. You will give your audience two sets of questions to answer: questions before viewing your Hero's Journey and questions after viewing your Hero's Journey. You must turn in the responses to the questions along with your final product (your Hero's Journey).

7. In a small group in World Studies on Thursday, June 6, you will do the following:

   1. Explain one of your challenges.
   2. Explain how you overcame your challenge.
   3. Compare your challenge to something that Odysseus faced.
   4. Compare your challenge to an aspect of the Hero's Journey.

● **RESOURCE A2.6** Benchmark Assignment

Artist's Statement

Due: Wednesday, 6/5/20

Objective: Please write at least a one paragraph artist's statement about your Hero's Journey Final Product.

Description of an Artist's Statement:

An **artist's statement** (or **artist statement**) is an artist's written description of their work. The goal is to give the viewer an understanding of your product. Your objective is to inform, connect with an art context, and present the basis for the work. The artist statement usually provides a description of the work, some indication of the work's art historical and theoretical context, some background information about the artist and the artist's intentions, technical specifications, and, at the same time, it aims to persuade the reader of the artwork's value.

Questions to Consider:

1. Why did you choose this medium?
2. Why did you choose these challenges?
3. What impressions do you hope the product makes on the audience?
4. Why did you choose the colors, lyrics, images, and the like for each challenge?
5. What does the audience see or hear?
6. What do you hope the audience walks away thinking?
7. What inspired you to make the creative decisions you chose?
8. What does this product represent or signify?
9. What does this product mean to you?
10. What else would you (the artist) like to add about your product?

● **RESOURCE A3.1** **12th-Grade Entrepreneurship Project Overview**

'Treps Care Too

Overview:

Entrepreneurialism today is mostly associated with innovation and financial gain; however, the mindset of an entrepreneur can just as easily be applied to social justice and leveraged for local community improvement. This project will ask you to embody an entrepreneurial mindset and apply Kolb's Experiential Learning Cycle to address one of two local community issues: homelessness or pedestrian safety. You will engage in data collection in the real world; use problem-solving, critical, and creative thinking skills; and ultimately apply all that you learn through this process in a final product and presentation.

DQ:

How can we leverage an entrepreneurial mindset to take action on a local community issue?

- How can we create a pedestrian and bike-friendly city of La Mesa? Specifically, how do we best address the student safety concerns on Highlander Way?
- How can we develop a supportive network within the city of La Mesa for the homeless population?

Benchmarks:

Stage: Concrete Experience, Observation & Reflection

- Conduct digital research.
- Conduct fieldwork for data collection.
- Deliverables: Infographic, Process Portfolio Part I

Stage: Abstract Conceptualization

- Participate in formal brainstorming session to "ideate."
- Seek out an "expert" and/or "end user" for feedback on your proposal.
- Deliverables: Solution Proposal, Process Portfolio Part II

Stage: Active Experimentation

- Engage in active experimentation and interact with those who are involved with the problem.
- Deliverables: Tangible Product to Show Solution, Feedback Results, Process Portfolio Part III

Stage: Final

- Deliverables: Write your recommendations to an authentic audience in a formal letter; Process Portfolio Part IV

Final Products:

- Digital Process Portfolio
  - Part I
    - Reflection
    - Fieldwork documentation with descriptions
    - Infographic as jpg/png
  - Part II
    - Reflection
    - Formal proposal of solution
  - Part III
    - Reflection
    - Documentation of final product
    - Documentation of seeking feedback on final product/solution

(Continued)

• RESOURCE A3.1 (Continued)

- o   Part IV
    - ▪   Final reflection
    - ▪   Documentation of presentation
- • Final presentation: Each student will need to invite an authentic expert to her or his presentation.
- • Refined prototype/product of solution based on feedback
- • Formal letter written, with recommendations, to authentic audience

Assessment:

- • Benchmark Assignments (40 points)
    - o   Thoroughness, meets due dates, reflection and revision
- • Process Portfolio (50 points)
    - o   Professional presentation, proper documentation, thorough reflection
- • Presentation (30 points)
    - o   Oral communication skills, preparation in presentation
- • Prototype/Final product (40 points)
    - o   Innovative design, displays feedback and revision
- • Formal Recommendations Letter (20 points)
    - o   Formal voice, supporting data, identification of authentic audience

• RESOURCE A3.2 12th-Grade Project Facilitation Notes

Day 1: Project Launch

- • Provide student overview.
- • Connection to ICE curriculum
    - o   pp. 54–56; challenge assumptions; see yourself as empowered advocates to reexamine old ideas
- • "Concrete Experience": Field work
    - o   Visit area on campus of concern.
    - o   Walk through downtown La Mesa.
    - o   Complete field notes (see Google Drive "Documenting Real-World Work").
    - o   Debrief the experience (see Google Drive "Debriefing Real-World Work").

Day 2: Identifying Problem

- • Connection to ICE
    - o   Problem = Opportunity (p. 62)
- • Students identify which topic they would like to research.
    - o   Consider creating a "project wall" in your classroom. You can write out all the benchmarks, and each group has a sticky note that they move when they are on that benchmark (this will really help you manage the process as groups start to fall behind). If you do this, have students write their topic on their sticky note with their name when they place it on the first column.

- Columns would be titled the names of each benchmark and the deliverables.
- You may also want to have a space in the room near this wall where students have team folders to keep all corresponding documentation and you also post the project overview and calendar.
  - Provide first reading on each topic (break into topic groups).
    - Homeless issue, additional report
    - Pedestrian safety—Have guest speaker come speak to group and project renderings.
    - Consider leading a small-group discussion after reading/guest speaker.
    - Perhaps use a visible thinking routine, or simply ask *"what can we assume about this problem"* and have them journal/record for Process Portfolio.
- Workshop: Intro ICE Opportunity Discovery Process (wrkbk p. 54)
- E4B Workshop: Research methods
  - Possible topics to cover—reliability, bias, documenting research
- Work time (both classes): Begin researching topic/"the problem"

Day 3: Researching Problem

- Workshop: Interviewing experts
  - See strategy in Google Drive ("Interviewing Experts").
- Research time (continue digital research)
- Due: Have students turn in their questions and data collection method for interviews.

Day 4: Field Work

- Interviews for data collection if needed
  - Be sure to have students document field work if they go (see Google Drive "Documenting Real-World Exploration").
  - Also will want to debrief their experience (see Google Drive "Debriefing Real-World Work").
- Continue digital research.

Day 5: Disseminating Research

- Warm up: Have students complete ICE workbook, p. 60.
- Workshop: How to create an infographic
  - Students will need to create an account on Piktochart or Easely. I recommend you do this process before showing students how to do it!
  - Review the infographic lesson/unit provided in Google Drive and decide how much of it you want to do.
  - Find student samples of infographics; I have about 6 images.

Day 6: Disseminating Research

- Work on infographics, research

Day 7: Digital Portfolio Development

- Workshop: Designing a Digital Portfolio
  - Note: For Benchmark #1, students will need to have documented the first part of the project with images, video, notes, links, and the like. They will also need to respond to a reflection that you will provide on the due date.

(Continued)

● **RESOURCE A3.2** (Continued)

Day 8: Work!

- Big work day

Day 9: Reflection Day

- Provide students with the following Process Portfolio Reflection:
  - On pp. 54–56 of our textbook, we learn about assumptions and the value of reexamining old ideas. While in the first two phases of Kolb's Experiential Learning Cycle, what assumptions did you make? How are you challenging yourself to reexamine old ideas related to the problems you are unearthing through this project?
- Due by end of class:
  - Infographic on DP
  - Process Portfolio Reflection on DP

Day 10: Brainstorming

- Solution brainstorming protocol
  - Consider a protocol from National School Reform Faculty or *Gamestorming* book.
  - You may also want to review norms first.
  - Complete p. 64 ICE.

Day 11: Writing Day

- E4B Workshop: Proposal writing

Day 12: Feedback

- Peer feedback on proposals
  - Use "Collaborative Feedback" strategy in Google Drive.
- Students to seek out expert for feedback on their proposed solution.

Day 13: Reflection Day

- Process Portfolio Reflection
  - In Chapter 1 of our textbook, the concepts of limitations, resilience, and breaking tradition are discussed. Reflect upon the ways in which you have displayed these traits throughout the second phase of this project.
- Due by end of class: Benchmark II (proposal, reflection)

Day 14: Brainstorming Day

- Brainstorm final product ideas to show solutions.
- You may need to provide some examples/models (e.g., blueprints, renderings, etc.).
- Revisit norms.
- Have students come up with three to five ideas and rank from there.
- You may consider pp. 68–69 of workbook.

Day 15: Catch-Up

- Possible workshops on how to design final products

Days 16–17: Work!

- Big work days
- Final product due by end of class on Day 17; have students document and upload pictures/graphics to Process Portfolio for Part III.
- Exit for the day: Process Portfolio Part III Reflection
  - We learn that "problem = opportunity." Discuss the ways in which that phrase applies to your solution and final product design.

Day 18: Workshop Preparation

- Workshop: Data collection methods
  - See "Collecting Data in the Real World" in Google Drive for plans.
  - Students will need to identify how they will seek feedback on their solution and final product.
  - Be sure students document the feedback they receive to upload to Process Portfolio.

Day 19: Workshop Review

- Workshop: Giving a formal presentation
  - Review assessment tool for presentation.

Days 20–21: Final Product Prep

- Presentation prep
  - Consider: "Peer Feedback for Oral Presentations" in Google Drive.
- Students will also simultaneously be seeking feedback on their solution and final product design.

Days 22–23: Presentations

- Consider using strategy in Google Drive ("Ensuring an Engaged Audience").
- Students may consider documenting presentation for Process Portfolio.

Day 24: Writing Day

- E4B workshop: Formal letter writing

Day 25: Work!

- Catch-up work day

Day 26: Revision Day

- Peer revision to letter
  - Consider "Collaborative Feedback" strategy in Google Drive.

Day 27: Last Day

- Final Day!
- Final Process Portfolio Reflection:
  - Consider this statement: "An entrepreneurial mindset requires us to be willing to push the limits of what we think we are capable of, to take personal risks, and to take action." Reflect on the ways in which you displayed an entrepreneurial mindset throughout this project.

• RESOURCE A3.3 12th-Grade Project Calendar

	Monday	Tuesday	Wednesday	Thursday	Friday
Phase I- Concrete Experience Observation & Reflection	5 Labor Day— No School	6 ICE Lesson 1 Review Wkshp: Intro to Kolb's Learning Cycle ICE Lesson 2 Part 1 Mult. Ch. Assessment	7 Project Launch (Mr. Osborn) Field Work-Observation (Helix Campus) E4B WKshp: Research	8 Field Work-Observation (Downtown La Mesa)	9 ICE House Lesson 2 Part 2 Mult. Choice Application (Use current problem) Reflection
	12 Wkshp: Interviewing Experts/ End-Users Due: Interview Prep	13 Field Work: Interviews	14 ICE p. 60 Wkshp: Infographic	15 Wkshp: Digital/ Process Portfolio Design	16 **ICE House Lesson 3 Part 1**
Phase II- Forming abstract concepts	19 **Due: Benchmark 1** (Process Portfolio I, Infographic)	20 E4B Wkshp: Proposal Writing Wkshp: Brainstorming Protocol ICE p. 64	21 Guest Speaker BE Movement Nate Howard	22 **Due: Benchmark 2** Peer, Expert Feedback on Proposal	23 Brainstorm Product to Show Solution
Phase III- Prototype	26 Potential Wkshp: Designing Final Products	27 Work Day	28 **Work Day**	29 Kristy Thompson City of La Mesa Expert/End User Interviews	30 Wkshp: Data Collection Methods Wkshp: Presentations
Phase IV- Test and Refine, Present	3 ICE House Lesson 3 Part 2	4 Work Day	5 **Work Day**	6 **3-D Models Due**	7 No School Staff Development Day
Phase V- Final Completion	10 Display Work Day	11 Display Work Day Expert Questions for Mayor	12 Field Work: Trip to Mayor's Office 11:00 am Amanda Rogers 619-667-1105	13 **Due: Letter Uploaded to IV**	14

● **RESOURCE A3.4** 12th-Grade Project Assessment Checklist

Process Portfolio

	Emerging	Proficient	Advanced
Professional Presentation: Voice is a professional tone; work is professionally presented, including no grammatical or spelling errors.			
Documentation: The entire process of learning is captured and shared via diverse forms of documentation (video, photos, captions, etc.).			
Reflection: Response to reflection prompts display depth of thinking, cited evidence of work, and growth throughout the learning process.			
Total Points Possible: **Total Points Received:**			

Proposal Presentation

	Emerging	Proficient	Advanced
Evidence of Primary Research: Student demonstrates ways in which expert interviews, digital research, and primary sources influenced changes in their project.			
Preparation: Visuals were utilized to enhance student presentation; student shows practice of presentation; organization is displayed in flow of presentation.			
Response to Q & A: Responds to questions in a professional manner; cites specific evidence for reasoning; engages with audience.			
Oral Communication Skills: Voice is projected; makes eye contact with audience; has a professional appearance; tone is engaging.			
Total Points Possible: **Total Points Received:**			

Prototype/Final Product

	Emerging	Proficient	Advanced
Ingenuity: Product displays a creative solution, resourcefulness, and innovative design.			
Improvement: Final product displays gains/improvement from initial prototype, as evidenced by response to feedback.			

(Continued)

Appendix A

● **RESOURCE A3.4** (Continued)

	Emerging	Proficient	Advanced
Response to Problem/Solution: Final product displays a clear connection to a problem and viable solution to community issue.			
Total Points Possible: **Total Points Received:**			

● **RESOURCE A4.1** Assessment Tips and Tricks From the Trenches

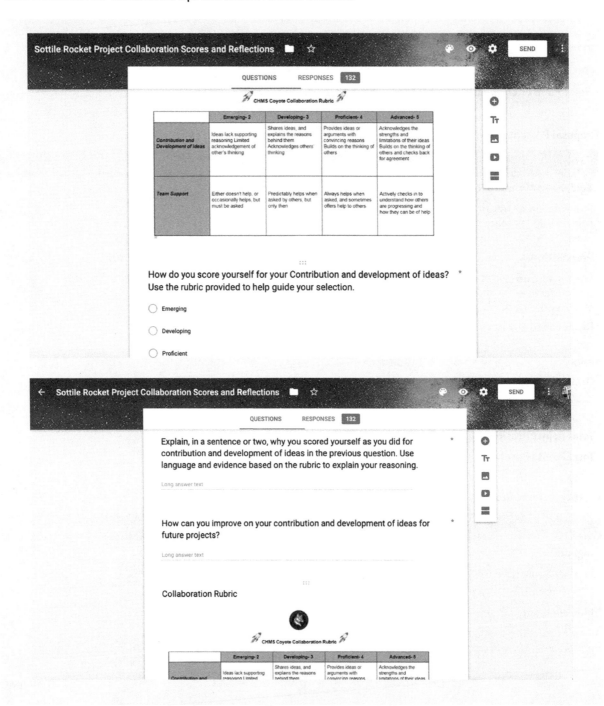

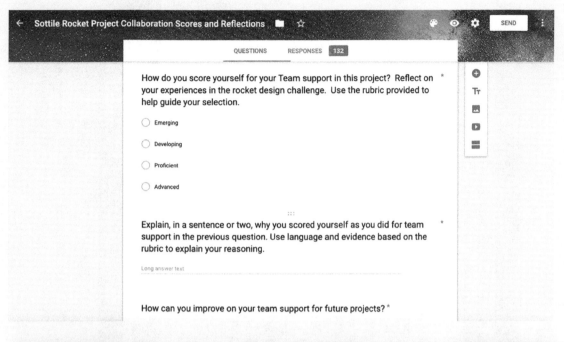

Sottile Rocket Project Collaboration Scores and Reflections

QUESTIONS   RESPONSES   132

How do you score yourself for your Team support in this project? Reflect on your experiences in the rocket design challenge. Use the rubric provided to help guide your selection. *

○ Emerging

○ Developing

○ Proficient

○ Advanced

Explain, in a sentence or two, why you scored yourself as you did for team support in the previous question. Use language and evidence based on the rubric to explain your reasoning. *

Long answer text

How can you improve on your team support for future projects? *

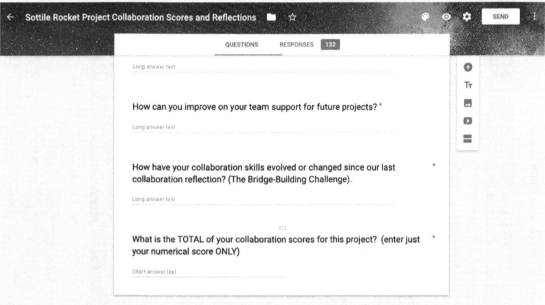

Sottile Rocket Project Collaboration Scores and Reflections

QUESTIONS   RESPONSES   132

Long answer text

How can you improve on your team support for future projects? *

Long answer text

How have your collaboration skills evolved or changed since our last collaboration reflection? (The Bridge-Building Challenge). *

Long answer text

What is the TOTAL of your collaboration scores for this project? (enter just your numerical score ONLY) *

Short answer text

Appendix A

• **RESOURCE A5.1 Sample Detailed Scope and Sequence for Ninth Grade**

Unit 1	Matter and Its Interactions
Major content understandings and applications	As a result of this unit, students will gain scientific knowledge of matter in order to explain the outcome of a (simple) chemical reaction. Students will then apply this newly acquired knowledge to an interdisciplinary project. This process will require that students display mastery of the following DCIs through various learning activities:

- Students will demonstrate understanding of the periodic table and patterns of chemical properties so they can make predictions and construct explanations for outcomes of chemical reactions. (HS-PS1-1, HS-PS1-2)
- Students will understand scientific principles of matter in order to develop an explanation about the effects of changing temperature or concentration of the reacting particles on the rate at which a reaction occurs. (HS-PS1-5)
- Students will engage in hands-on investigations to gather evidence in order to compare the structure of substances at the Buk scale to infer the strength of electrical forces between particles. (HS-PS1-3)
- Students will demonstrate their understanding of bond energy and its impact on chemical reactions by creating a model of this process. (HS-PS1-4)
- Students will understand how a change in conditions could produce increased amounts of products at equilibrium and will show this understanding by refining the design of a chemical system. (Ps-PS1-6)
- Students will be able to use mathematical ideas to communicate the proportional relationships between masses of atoms in the reactants and the products and the translation of these relationships to the macroscopic scale using the mole as the conversion, so they can fully explain reactivity. (Hs-PS1-7)

Driving Question	How do properties of matter explain their interactions?
Duration	5–7 weeks

Science Content and Skills	Additional Skills	Assessment	Differentiation Spotlight	Interdisciplinary Connections	IPSO Approach in Action
Science and Engineering Practices:	Oral Communication:	Formative:	ELL:	CCSS ELA:	Social Justice/ Equity:
	• Verbal defense of method	• Technical literacy	• Technical literacy	• RST. 11-12.1 • WHST.	• Heterogeneous grouping

Appendix B

Blank Project Planning Forms

 The following project planning forms can also be found on the companion website at **resources.corwin.com/keepitrealPBLsecondary**.

The PBL Brainstorming Planning Form is designed to capture your wild and crazy ideas. This is not the place to get married to any particular idea; it is simply a place to organize your thoughts and start to make some connections. If you come up with a big idea but can't connect it to any standard you need to cover, scratch that idea and start with a new line of thinking.

PBL Brainstorming Planning Form

Big ideas

These topics should be related to content areas for your grade level.

Real-world context

How does this relate to an authentic problem that is relevant to your community/students?

Standards and skills

What standards can you see connecting to your idea?

Final product

What can students create/do/share?

Potential real-world connection

Who might you bring in? Where might you take students out?

Source: © 2018 Jennifer Pieratt.

Download a blank version of this template at resources.corwin.com/keepitrealPBLsecondary

Complete the top of this form (EU, standards/skills, DQ, final product, culminating experience) to figure out how to organize the building blocks of your project.

Project Planner

Title: Grade:

Content Area:

Enduring Understanding:

Standards and Skills:

Driving Question:

Final Product:

Culminating Experience:

Benchmark Phases: Student Deliverables:

1.   1.

2.   2.

3.   3.

Use the template provided to help you build your rubric. List relevant twenty-first century skills in the far left and then copy/paste the corresponding text as needed.

Project Rubric Template

21st-Century Skill	Emerging–Developing (1–2)	Proficient (3)	Advanced (4)

Use the template provided by referencing your teacher-facing rubric and rewriting each row as a learning target in student-friendly language.

Student Project Rubric Template

	Not Yet	Most of the Time	Always
I can …			
I can …			
I can …			
I can …			
I can …			
I can …			
I can …			
I can …			

Source: Adapted from PBLWorks Presentation Rubric ©2011.

Download a blank version of this template at resources.corwin.com/keepitrealPBLsecondary

CraftED
Group Game Plan

Project:

Group Assignment:

Names	Contact Information
1.	
2.	
3.	
4.	
5.	

As a group, we hope to . . .

A strength each person brings to this group is . . .

A worry or fear each person has about working together/this project is . . .

Some challenges we may face during this project are . . .

If we run into these challenges, we will . . .

We will make decisions by . . .

As a group, we agree to . . .

If a group member is not upholding this game plan, as a group we will . . .

Student Name	Signature	Parent	Teacher

Source: ©2018 Jennifer Piearatt

Download this template at resources.corwin.com/keepitrealPBLsecondary

Glossary

Agency: Agency is defined by Hitlin and Elder (2007) by four overlapping concepts, two of which apply to being an adult learner in PBL:

1) Identity agency: What we believe about ourselves and the ways that we wish to be perceived by others
2) Life-course agency: Actions that we take to affect future outcomes

To learn more about the definition of agency and how it relates to PBL, visit the companion website (www.resources.corwin.com/keepitrealPBL) or Chapter 2.

Driving Questions (DQ): A driving question is the big question that guides student learning throughout the course of the project. The DQ is student-facing and helps address the daily question "Why are we learning this?" The DQ also helps make a connection between what students are learning and your enduring understanding (EU) because the two are directly related. For more, see Chapter 5.

Driving Standards: Driving standards lead the project planning because they more easily provide a context for project learning. Typically, driving standards concern social studies/history or science. See Chapter 4 for more.

Enduring Understanding (EU): EU is a simple teacher-facing statement that serves as the "umbrella," or big idea, for planning; it is rooted in your standards. See Chapter 5 for more.

High-Quality Project-Based Learning (HQPBL): Created by a steering committee of leaders of the PBL movement, the definition of high-quality project-based learning includes the following:

- Intellectual challenge and accomplishment: Students learn deeply, think critically, and strive for excellence.
- Authenticity: Students work on projects that are meaningful and relevant to their culture, their lives, and their future.
- Public Product: Students' work is publicly displayed, discussed, and critiqued.
- Collaboration: Students collaborate with other students in person or online and/or receive guidance from adult mentors and experts.
- Project Management: Students use a project management process that enables them to proceed effectively from project initiation to completion.
- Reflection: Students reflect on their work and their learning throughout the project.

See Chapter 1 for more about HQPBL.

Integrated, Interdisciplinary Projects: Integrated projects are those that have a similar broad theme across content areas (e.g., water, relationships, cause/effect, etc.). Interdisciplinary projects truly use multiple content areas to enhance the completion of a project and equally depend on an understanding of all content areas involved in order to complete the project. See Chapter 4 for more.

Need to Knows (NTKs): This is a process that starts during the project launch and is revisited every day to guide student-driven learning and teacher instruction. During a project launch, students are provided time to consider what they know about the topic or process of the project, as well as what they need to know. Students share out their responses, and they are recorded and revisited throughout the project. To learn more, check out Chapter 10.

Power Standards: Ainsworth and Reeves (2004) define power standards as those that are essential rather than nice to know (see Chapter 4 for more). Power standards possess the following criteria:

- Long-term value ("endurance")
- Leverage, meaning it will be of value to multiple disciplines
- Readiness for the next level of learning (because they are essential skills needed for the following grade level or next level of instruction)

See Chapter 4 for more about power standards.

Problem-Based Learning (PrBL): Math expert Geoff Krall (2018) explains: "Similar to problem-based learning, project-based learning ties the content to a real-world context by providing the challenge that makes the math content necessary. The key differences between the two are the length of time required and the level of authenticity [or real-world connectedness]" (p. 87). Typically, in PrBL a unit includes one or two standards over a shorter amount of time than a project (1–3 days), and the emphasis is on the process and skills rather than a finished product. See Chapter 1 for more.

Project-Based Learning (PBL): [An experience in which] "students are pulled through the curriculum by a meaningful question to explore, an engaging real-world problem to solve, or a challenge to design or create something. . . . To demonstrate what they learn, students create high-quality products to present their work to other people" (Hallermann, Larmer, & Mergendoller, 2016, p. 5). See Chapter 1 for more.

References

Ainsworth, L. (with Reeves, D. B.). (2014). *Power standards: Identifying the standards that matter the most.* Englewood, CO: Advanced Learning Press.

Battelle for Kids. (2019). Framework for 21st century learning. Retrieved December 6, 2018, from http://www.p21.org/our-work/p21-framework

Boaler, J., & Confer, A. (n.d.). *Assessment for a growth mindset* (Rep.). Retrieved November 15, 2018, from https://docplayer.net/34446261-Assessment-for-a-growth-mindset-jo-boaler-amanda-confer-stanford-university.html.

Boss, S., & Larmer, J. (2018). *Project based teaching.* Alexandria, VA: ASCD.

Brookhart, S. (2016). *Rubrics for formative assessment and grading (quick reference guide).* Alexandria, VA: ASCD.

Christie, A. (with Todd, C.). (2013). *Hercule Poirot: The complete short stories.* New York, NY: HarperCollins.

DeSilver, D. (2017, February 15). U.S. academic achievement lags that of many other countries. Retrieved December 6, 2018, from http://www.pewresearch.org/fact-tank/2017/02/15/u-s-students-internationally-math-science/.

Dewey, J. (1938). *Experience and education.* New York, NY: MacMillian.

Gray, D., Brown, S., & Macanufo, J. (2010). *Gamestorming.* Sebastopol, CA: O'Reilly Media.

Hallermann, S., Larmer, J., & Mergendoller, J. R. (2016). *PBL in the elementary grades: Step-by-step guidance, tools and tips for standards-focused K–5 projects.* Novato, CA: Buck Institute for Education.

Hammond, Z. (with Jackson, Y.). (2015). *Culturally responsive teaching and the brain: Promoting authentic engagement and rigor among culturally and linguistically diverse students.* Thousand Oaks, CA: Corwin.

Hansen, M., Mann, E., Quintero, D., & Valant, J. (2018, April 17). Have we made progress on achievement gaps? Looking at evidence from the new NAEP results. Retrieved November 15, 2018, from https://www.brookings.edu/blog/brown-center-chalkboard/2018/04/17/have-we-made-progress-on-achievement-gaps-looking-at-evidence-from-the-new-naep-results/.

Hitlin, S., & Elder, G. H. (2007). Time, self, and the curiously abstract concept of agency. *Sociological Theory, 25*(2), 170–191. Retrieved from https://doi.org/10.1111/j.1467-9558.2007.00303.x.

Jamrisko, M., & Lu, W. (2018, January 22). The U.S. drops out of the top 10 in innovation ranking. *Bloomberg.com.* Retrieved from https://www.bloomberg.com/news/articles/2018-01-22/south-korea-tops-global-innovation-ranking-again-as-u-s-falls.

Krall, G. (2012, May 24). "Isn't problem-based learning easier than project-based learning? " *and 10 other myths about PrBL ("real or not real")* [Blog post]. Retrieved December 10, 2018, from https://emergentmath.com/2012/05/24/isnt-problem-based-learning-easier-than-project-based-learning-and-10-other-myths-about-prbl-real-or-not-real/.

Krall, G. (2018). *Necessary conditions: Teaching secondary math with academic safety, quality tasks, and effective facilitation*. Portland, ME: Stenhouse.

Larmer, J. (2016a, March 7). Research brief: What can we learn from John Hattie about project-based teaching?—Part 1 [Blog post]. Retrieved December 6, 2018, from http://www.bie.org/blog/what_can_we_learn_from_john_hattie_about_project_based_teaching_part_1.

Larmer, J. (2016b, March 29). Research brief: What can we learn from John Hattie about project-based teaching?—Part 2 [Blog post]. Retrieved December 6, 2018, from https://www.bie.org/blog/what_can_we_learn_from_john_hattie_about_project_based_teaching_part_2.

Larmer, J., & Mergendoller, J. R. (2010). *The main course, not dessert: How are students reaching 21st century goals? With 21st century project based learning*. Novato, CA: Buck Institute for Education.

McTighe, J., & Wiggins, G. (2012). *Understanding by design framework* (Rep.) Retrieved from https://www.ascd.org/ASCD/pdf/siteASCD/publications/UbD_WhitePaper0312.pdf.

Next Generation Science Standards. (n.d.). Evidence statements. Retrieved from https://www.nextgenscience.org/evidence-statements.

Next Generation Science Standards. (2013). How to read the *Next Generation Science Standards (NGSS)* [Press release]. Retrieved from https://www.nextgenscience.org/sites/default/files/How%20to%20Read%20NGSS%20-%20Final%204-19-13.pdf.

Next Generation Science Standards. (2015). K–5 ETS evidence statements June 2015 asterisks.pdf. Retrieved from https://www.nextgenscience.org/sites/default/files/evidence_statement/black_white/K-5%20ETS%20Evidence%20Statements%20June%202015%20asterisks.pdf.

Pieratt, J. R. (2011). *Teacher–student relationships in project based learning: A case study of High Tech Middle North County* (Doctoral dissertation). Retrieved from http://scholarship.claremont.edu/cgu_etd/13. (Paper 13)

Pieratt, J. R. (2019). Integrating the question formulation technique in PBL through the launch. *Right Question Institute*. Retrieved from https://rightquestion.org/resources/integrating-the-question-formulation-technique-in-pbl-through-the-launch/.

Reagan, M. (2015, April 9). Unpacking effective project based learning [Blog post]. *Corwin Connect*. Retrieved from https://corwin-connect.com/2015/04/unpacking-effective-project-based-learning/.

Sinek, S. (2009). *Simon Sinek: The golden circle—TED talks 2009* [Video file]. Retrieved from https://www.youtube.com/watch?v=fMOlfsR7SMQ.

Soep, E. L. (2008, Fall). Learning as production, critique as assessment. *UnBoxed*, 2. Retrieved from http://gse.hightechhigh.org/unboxed/issue2/learning_as_production/.

U.S. Department of Education. (n.d.). College- and career-ready standards. Retrieved December 6, 2018, from https://www.ed.gov/k-12reforms/standards.

Vincent, T. (2014, October 10). Crafting questions that drive projects [Blog post]. Retrieved December 6, 2018, from https://learninginhand.com/blog/drivingquestions.

Wagner, T. (2015). *Most likely to succeed: Preparing our kids for the innovation era*. New York, NY: Scribner. Retrieved from https://edcentral.uk/edblog/expert-insight/a-beginners-guide-tony-wagner.

Wisconsin Department of Public Instruction. (n.d.). Rubrics for classroom science assessment. Retrieved December 6, 2018, from https://dpi.wi.gov/science/assessment/rubrics/.

Wylie, C., & Lyon, C. (2016). *Using the formative assessment rubrics, reflection and observation tools to support professional reflection on practice* (Rev.). Retrieved from https://cms.azed.gov/home/GetDocumentFile?id=59495f623217e10fbc43eb0d.

Index

Confident Teachers, Inspired Learners

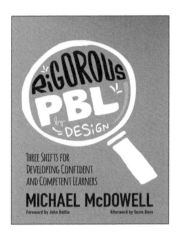

MICHAEL MCDOWELL

Find out how to make three shifts essential to improving PBL's overall effect by helping students discover, deepen, and then apply their learning to a world beyond them.

MICHAEL MCDOWELL

Building upon the groundwork from *Rigorous PBL by Design*, this resource provides practices that strategically support students as they move from novices to experts in core academics.

WILLIAM N. BENDER

This book's collection of instructional strategies and assessment methods shows how to implement and differentiate project-based learning that fosters 21st century skills in Grades K–12.

JANE KRAUSS AND SUZIE BOSS

Whether you are new to project-based learning or ready to strengthen your existing classroom projects, you'll find a full suite of strategies and tools in this essential book.

No matter where you are in your professional journey, Corwin aims to ease the many demands teachers face on a daily basis with accessible strategies that benefit ALL learners. Through research-based, high-quality content, we offer practical guidance on a wide range of topics, including curriculum planning, learning frameworks, classroom design and management, and much more. Our books, videos, consulting, and online resources are developed by renowned educators and designed for easy implementation that will provide tangible results for you and your students.

JENNIFER PIERATT

Written for busy teachers with realistic challenges in mind, this interactive, visually accessible guide introduces a clear and efficient process for planning enriching project-based learning units.

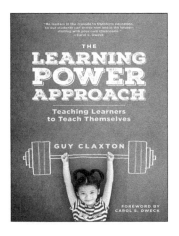

GUY CLAXTON

Understand how "every lesson, every day" shapes the way students see themselves as learners.

BARBARA BRAY AND KATHLEEN MCCLASKEY

Transform education so every learner is valued. Build a shared vision that supports personalized learning using the Universal Design for Learning (UDL) framework.

BARBARA BRAY AND KATHLEEN MCCLASKEY

This thorough and timely resource draws from Universal Design for Learning principles to create a powerful shift in classroom dynamics, guiding learners to become self-directed and self-motivated.

TMN19B80

A SAGE Publishing Company

Helping educators make the greatest impact

CORWIN HAS ONE MISSION: to enhance education through intentional professional learning.

We build long-term relationships with our authors, educators, clients, and associations who partner with us to develop and continuously improve the best evidence-based practices that establish and support lifelong learning.